IMITATING GOD – STUDY GUIDE

Therefore be imitators of God, as beloved children; and walk in love, just as Christ also loved you and gave Himself up for us . . .

Ephesians 5:1, 2

IMITATING GOD
STUDY GUIDE

*THE AMAZING SECRET OF
LIVING HIS LIFE*

Ruthven J. Roy

Rehoboth
PUBLISHING

Unless otherwise indicated, all Scripture quotations are taken from the *New American Standard Bible,* © 1960, 1962, 1963, 1968, 1971, 1972, 1973, 1975, 1977, by The Lockman Foundation. Used by permission.

Other versions used are
KJV – *The Authorized King James Version,* © 1975 by Thomas Nelson Inc., Publishers.
NIV – Scriptures taken from the *Holy Bible, New International Version.* © 1973, 1978, 1984 by International Bible Society. Used by permission of Zondervan Publishing House. All rights reserved.
NRSV – Scriptures taken from the *Holy Bible, New Revised Standard Version,* © 1989, by Division of Christian Education of the National Council of the Churches of Christ in the United States of America.

Imitating God Study Guide – Study Guide: The Amazing Secret of Living His Life
Copyright © 2010 by Ruthven J. Roy

ISBN: Paperback   978-0-9717853-6-6
                                         0-9717853-6-8

Printed in the United States of America. **All rights reserved.** No part of this book may be reproduced or transmitted in any form or by any means without written permission from the publisher.

Rehoboth Publishing, LLC
P.O. Box 33
Berrien Springs, MI 49103

For additional copies of this book or for author speaking engagements write to:
ruthvenroy@networkdiscipling.org, or visit www.networkdiscipling.org

Imitating God – Study Guide

Table of Contents

How to Use This Study Guide.. VII

It's All About Identity 11

Chapter 1	*In the Beginning*
	• Outline.. 13
	• Leader's Notes.. 16
	• Review Questions... 18
	• Answer Key.. 21
	• Scriptural References... 22

Chapter 2	*Ultimate Makeover – The Spiritual Edition*
	• Outline.. 25
	• Leader's Notes.. 29
	• Review Questions... 31
	• Answer Key.. 34
	• Scriptural References... 35

Chapter 3	*Designed for Success*
	• Outline.. 39
	• Leader's Notes.. 42
	• Review Questions... 44
	• Answer Key.. 47
	• Scriptural References... 48

Chapter 4	*Bridging the Gap*
	• Outline.. 51
	• Leader's Notes.. 55
	• Review Questions... 57
	• Answer Key.. 60
	• Scriptural References... 61

Training the Inner Spirit-Man..65

    Chapter 5   *Learning to Hear Again*
- Outline..67
- Leader's Notes...69
- Review Questions..70
- Answer Key..72
- Scriptural References...73

    Chapter 6   *Learning to See Again*
- Outline..75
- Leader's Notes...77
- Review Questions..78
- Answer Key..80
- Scriptural References..81

    Chapter 7   *Learning to Speak Again*
- Outline..85
- Leader's Notes...88
- Review Questions..90
- Answer Key..93
- Scriptural References..94

    Chapter 8   *Learning to Walk Again*
- Outline..97
- Leader's Notes...101
- Review Question..103
- Answer Key..106
- Scriptural References...108

Like Father, Like Son..113

    Chapter 9   *Living God's Life*
- Outline..115
- Leader's Notes...120
- Review Questions..122
- Answer Key..125
- Scriptural References...126

Imitating God – Study Guide

How to Use This Study Guide

This *Study Guide* is designed to help you maximize the benefits you will receive from studying **Imitating God**. Whether you are studying for deeper intimacy with your heavenly Father, leading a small group, or training disciples for kingdom service, you will find this *Study Guide* a needed, user-friendly companion for accomplishing all of the above objectives. Here is how it works:

Each unit is made up of five sections—namely, the <u>Chapter Outline</u>, <u>Leader's Notes</u>, <u>Review Questions</u>, <u>Answer Key</u> and <u>Scriptural References</u>.

Small Group or Disciple Training

The facilitator or leader of the group should encourage and require each group member or disciple to read the proposed chapter for the assigned study before reporting to the group or training session.

During the session, the leader simply facilitates the study using the <u>Leader's Notes</u>, while the group follows along using the <u>Chapter Outline</u>. Except for additional details, questions and answers, the <u>Leader's Notes</u> follows the same path as the Chapter Outline.

The leader, therefore, should review one numbered section at a time, and ask all group members or disciples to locate and read aloud all scriptures pertaining to that section. Feel free to entertain questions and/or discussions that pertain to the scripture and text of each of the numbered sections, without permitting foreign ideas (irrelevant to the study at hand), caustic argumentation, or dominating personalities to railroad the lesson. The leader's goal should be to involve everyone in the teaching and learning process, so that all may have the opportunity to gain a proper understanding of the study material.

The <u>Review Questions</u> are provided for crystallizing students' understanding of the Biblical principles and concepts they received during the study. These should be assigned as "homework" at the end of each session, which should be reviewed at the beginning of the next group meeting.

Most of the *Scriptural References* of the *Study Guide* are taken from the *New American Standard* version of the Bible.

Brief Outline:

1. Connect with previous study by going over *Review Questions* ("homework") and *Answer Key*.

2. Facilitate group study or training session with the *Leader's Notes*.

    (a) Be sure that each participant has a copy of the *Chapter Outline*.
    (b) Encourage each one to follow along as you read the *Leader's Notes*.
    (c) Cover one numbered section at a time.
    (d) Have all participants read the scriptures for each section.
    (e) Facilitate healthy, relevant questions/discussion pertaining to Scriptures and individual section.
    (f) Repeat the process for every other numbered section.

3. Distribute copies of *Review Questions* to be completed at home.

Materials Needed: **Study Guide**, BIBLE, and enough copies of the ***Lesson Outline*** and ***Review Questions*** for each participant.

Personal Study

For personal study, the disciple is encouraged to read through the chapter in the main text, **Imitating God**, and review the *Leader's Notes*. Then, answer all the *Review Questions*. Check the *Answer Key* to evaluate your responses. Make the necessary corrections (if any) to your answers. Be sure to review all *Scriptural References* to maximize the benefit from your study.

Remember: The *Answer Key* is not provided as a "cheat sheet" to be used before the reading of the main text (**Imitating God**) and the *Leader's Notes*. This provision is made for you to evaluate and confirm your personal understanding of each chapter of **Imitating God**, with the view that you would eventually live the life that your heavenly Father has designed for you. Therefore, to your own self be true.

Brief Outline:

Read chapter in **Imitating God**.
Search out all Scriptural References.

Review *Leader's Notes*.
Answer *Review Questions*.
Evaluate your responses by checking *Answer Key*.

Materials Needed: *Imitating God, Study Guide*, BIBLE, writing stationery and pen/pencil.

PART I

IT'S ALL ABOUT IDENTITY

But He [Jesus] continued, "*You are from below; I am from above. You are of this world; I am not of this world.*"

John 8:23, NIV

But our citizenship is in heaven. And we eagerly await a Savior from there, the Lord Jesus Christ.

Philippians 3:20

IN THE BEGINNING

Chapter 1 – Outline

In the beginning <u>was the Word</u>, and <u>the Word was with God</u>, and <u>the Word was God</u>. The same [Word] was in the beginning with God. <u>All things were made by Him</u>; and without Him was not anything made that was made.

John 1:1-3

1. **Our planet is a Word creation**

    By the word of the Lord were the heavens made, and all the hosts of them by the breath of His mouth. . . He spake [spoke], and it was done; He commanded, and it stood fast [firm] (Psalm 33:6, 9).

    A. Christ is the Word-Creator who was in the beginning with God, the Father and the Holy Spirit.

    B. The creative force of "God said" occurs nine times in Genesis 1.

    C. Everything on our planet was created by words and is sustained by the same.

    D. God places very high priority on the words that proceed from His mouth.

2. **Created in God's image and likeness**

    A. Mankind is also a word product, just like the rest of the creation.

    B. Image and likeness had no relation to man's external clay form.

    C. God's image and likeness was in God's spirit life which He breathed into man.

    D. Man was created to be an extension of God.

3. ***What is man, that thou art mindful of him? and the son of man, that thou visitest him? ⁵For thou hast made him a little lower than the angels, and hast crowned him with glory and honour. ⁶Thou madest him to have dominion over the works of thy hands; thou hast put all things under his feet: (Psalm 8:4-6).***

   A. Man comprises spirit, soul and body, but functions as an indivisible unit (1 Thessalonians 5:23).

   B. Man's spirit expresses his God-consciousness, his soul reflects his self-consciousness, and his body projects his world-consciousness.

   C. Man's spirit was formed within him at his creation (Nehemiah 12:1).

   D. Unlike the angels, man is a ruling embodied spirit being.

   E. Christ, the last Adam, was also an embodied Spirit, who through His life and death became linked forever with the human family.

4. **The tree of the knowledge of good and evil was the devil's deceptive masterpiece to secure the allegiance of man through disobedience.**

   A. Lucifer was the first I-man. "I" is the hallmark of self-centeredness and sin.

   B. God alone is the supreme "I" in the universe. He alone has the power and authority to be the great **I AM**.

   C. The tree of the knowledge of good and evil was planted by the enemy of God, and stood in direct opposition to everything represented by the tree of life.

   D. The Creator (Christ) said that one can either make a tree good and its fruit good, or a tree evil and its fruit evil; but never a tree bearing good and evil at the same time (Matthew 12:33).

   E. Through the tree of the knowledge of good and evil, the devil sowed the seed of doubt and self-centered rebellion in humankind.

   F. Through this tree, the arch-deceiver's purpose was to move the center of man's decision-making from his heart (inner spirit-life that directly connected him to God) to his head; from trusting God to trusting self and reason.

5. **Man lost his identity, dominion and authority through his fall in the Garden of Eden.**

    A. When man sinned, his spirit was separated from the life of God (the Great Spirit), and he became filled with guilt and shame.

    B. As a result, human beings continually try to hide their guilt and shame by shifting blame on others, or on their situation.

    C. He, who was given dominion and rule by his Maker, now realized that he was the subject of another power, and that he had lost control of the creation that once obeyed him.

    D. Mankind turned from God to himself to answer all his questions, and to find all the solutions to the problems of his sinful life.

    E. Driven by the emptiness of his misguided soul, man began identifying himself by all sorts of vain philosophies, ideologies, deviant behaviors and lifestyles.

    F. The Earth has become a planet of shadow-chasers as mankind tries to retrieve what he has lost on account of the fall.

    G. Divine intervention prevented the human race from falling under the complete dominion of evil one.

IN THE BEGINNING

Lesson 1 – Leader's Notes

1. Our earth is called a "word" planet because it was created by the spoken word of God. God spoke everything into existence, and nothing was created without God speaking it first. Nine times in the Genesis account we encounter the clause "God said," as the whole of creation unfolded. The effect of God's speaking was both immediate and continuous. Whatever God spoke, came into existence, and continues to operate to this very day within the limits established by His authoritative word. Moreover, the God who spoke the creation into being is also called the "Word," who became flesh and lived among us (John 1:1-4, 14). He is the one who made all things and hold them in place by the power of His word (Colossians 1:16-19).

2. Mankind is also a word product, for his existence was spoken before He was formed from the dust of the ground (Genesis 1:26; 2:7). He was created in the image and likeness of God. This image and likeness had no material relation to his external clay form, but resided only in God's life in his spirit and the expression of that life through the activities of his soul or personhood.

3. The total man comprises of the indivisible elements of his spirit, soul and body (Zechariah 12:1; Numbers 16:22; 1 Thessalonians 5:23). Through his spirit, he achieves his God-consciousness; his soul reflects his self-consciousness or personhood; and by his body he experiences contact with the world about him—that is, his world-consciousness. Unlike the angels, who were made disembodied, ministering spirits, mankind was created a ruling, embodied spirit and given dominion over all creation. The last Adam (Christ) bore marked resemblance to the first Adam in that His existence was also spoken by the angel Gabriel before He was born, and He too was a ruling, embodied spirit—spirit in a fleshly body (Luke 1:30-35).

4. The tree of the knowledge of good and evil was the devil's deceptive masterpiece which he planted and used to secure man's loyalty to further his rebellion against his Maker. Only the enemy of God would plant a tree that yield a fruit that is both evil and good at the same time (Matthew 12:33;

7:17-20). This tree represented everything that God was not, a symbol of self-centeredness and all that is in the world—the lust of the flesh, the lust of the eye and the pride of life. Its nature is to foster an existence completely independent of God and his perfect will for all creation. This tree became the acid test of man's allegiance to God, and the flowing fountain to feed the seed of rebellion the enemy had implanted in his soul.

5. Through artful deception, the devil succeeded in persuading man to sin against his Creator. Because of his disobedience towards God, man lost his identity, domain and his sovereign rule over the rest of creation. Reason replaced the authority of the word of God as the locus for making decisions regarding God's will and purpose for human existence. Disconnection from his Maker plunged the race in an identity crisis from which it was impossible to extricate itself without divine intervention.

IN THE BEGINNING

Lesson 1 – Review Questions

1. Why our world is called *a* "word" planet?

   _____

   _____

2. What is the significance of the title "Word-God"? Who does this title refer to and why?

   _____

   _____

3. Why is man called a "word" product?

   _____

   _____

4. What is the breath of life?

   _____

   _____

5. What three elements comprise total man?

   _____

   _____

6. In what way was man an expression of God's image and likeness?

   _____
   _____

7. What basic characteristic did the next-generation Adam share with the first Adam?

   _____
   _____

8. Why was the devil able to perch as a serpent on the tree of the knowledge of good and evil?

   _____
   _____

9. What scriptures did Jesus quote that gave a hint to the truth about who really planted the tree of the knowledge of good and evil?

   _____
   _____

10. The Tree of Life is a representation of . . .

    _____

11. What did the tree of the knowledge of good and evil represent?

    _____
    _____

12. What intrinsic character traits does the fallen race share with Lucifer?

_____

_____

13. How did the fall of man affect his understanding concerning his true identity?

_____

_____

The Imitation of God – Study Guide

IN THE BEGINNING

Lesson 1 – Answer Key

1. It came into existence by the spoken word of God.

2. The "Word" is another name for God, the Creator. Jesus.

3. Man's existence was spoken before he came to be.

4. God's quickening spirit of divine consciousness which gave life to the clay form of man.

5. Spirit, Soul and Body.

6. In his spirit, man bore the divine imprint of his Creator. Through his soul he was able to express attributes akin to God.

7. They were both embodied spirits—that is, spirit-life in a body of flesh.

8. Because he is the one who really planted it.

9. Matthew 7:17-20; 12:33. Christ, the Creator, said that a tree and its fruits could either be made good or evil, but never good and evil at the same time.

10. God-dependence or complete trust in God; God-centeredness.

11. Life independent of God—that is self-dependence. All that is in the world—lust of the flesh, lust of the eye and the pride of life (1 John 2:16).

12. Pride and self-centeredness.

13. Man began identifying himself totally by his soul life or natural self-existence.

IN THE BEGINNING

Lesson 1 – Important Scriptures

In the beginning <u>was the Word</u>, and <u>the Word was with God</u>, and <u>the Word was God</u>. The same [Word] was in the beginning with God. <u>All things were made by Him</u>; and without Him was not anything made that was made.
John 1:1-3

by <u>the word</u> of the Lord were the heavens made, and all the hosts of them by the breath of His mouth. . . <u>He spake</u> [spoke], and it was done; <u>He commanded</u>, and it stood fast.
Psalm 33:6, 9, KJV

"It is the Spirit who gives life; the flesh profits nothing. The words I have spoken unto you are spirit and they are life."
John 6:63

[16]"For by him all things were created: things in heaven and on earth, visible and invisible, whether thrones or powers or rulers or authorities; all things were created by him and for him. [17]He is before all things, and in him all things hold together. [18]And he is the head of the body, the church; he is the beginning and the firstborn from among the dead, so that in everything he might have the supremacy. [19]For God was pleased to have all his fullness dwell in him . . ."
Colossians 1:16-19, NIV

[26]*And <u>God said</u>, Let us make man in <u>our image</u>, after <u>our likeness</u>: and <u>let them have dominion</u> over the fish of the sea, and over the fowl of the air, and over the cattle, and over all the earth, and over every creeping thing that creepeth upon the earth.* [27]*So God created man in his own image, in the image of God created he him; male and female created he them.*
Genesis 1:26, 27

And the LORD God formed man of the dust of the ground, and breathed into his nostrils the <u>breath of life</u>; and man became a <u>living soul</u>.
Genesis 2:7, KJV

"Thus declares the LORD who stretches out the heavens, lays the foundation of the earth, and <u>forms the spirit of man within him</u>",
Zechariah 12:1

"it is <u>the spirit in a man</u>, <u>the breath of the Almighty</u>, that gives him understanding."
Job 32:8, NIV

The spirit of man is the lamp of the Lord, searching the innermost parts of his belly.
Proverbs 20:27

"And the very God of peace sanctify you wholly; and I pray God your whole <u>spirit</u> and <u>soul</u> and <u>body</u> be preserved blameless unto the coming of our Lord Jesus Christ".
1 Thessalonians 5:23

^{4}What is man, that thou art mindful of him . . . ? ^{5}For thou hast made him <u>a little lower than the angels</u>, and hast <u>crowned him with glory and honour</u>. ^{6}Thou madest him to <u>have dominion</u> over the works of thy hands; <u>thou hast put all things under his feet</u>:
Psalm 8:4-6

^{31}"And behold, you will conceive in your womb and bear a son, and <u>you shall name Him Jesus</u>. ^{32}<u>He</u> will be great and <u>will be called the Son of the Most High</u>; and the Lord God will give Him the throne of His father David; ^{33}and He will reign over the house of Jacob forever, and His kingdom will have no end. . . ^{35}The Holy Spirit will come upon you, and the power of the Most High will overshadow you; and for that reason the holy Child shall be called the Son of God."
Luke 1:31-35

Either make a tree good, and its fruit good; or make the tree bad, and its fruit bad; for the tree is known by its fruit.

Matthew 12:33

. . . every good tree bringeth forth good fruit; but a corrupt tree bringeth forth evil fruit. [18]<u>A good tree <u>cannot bring forth evil fruit</u></u>, neither can a corrupt tree bring forth good fruit. [19]Every tree that bringeth not forth good fruit is hewn down, and cast into the fire. [20]Wherefore by their fruits ye shall know them.

Matthew 7:17-20, KJV

ULTIMATE MAKEOVER: THE SPIRITUAL EDITION

Chapter 2 – Outline

"Therefore, if anyone is in Christ, he is a new creation; the old has gone, the new has come!"

2 Corinthians 5:17, NIV

1. **God is the ultimate reconstruction Artist**

    A. God will make a new creation of anyone who receives Jesus as Savior and Lord.

    B. This new creation is a spiritual regeneration in which God's Spirit breathes new life in the depraved spirit of the Adam man.

    C. This new inner spirit-man is the dwelling place of the Holy Spirit who fulfills all the blessings of the New Covenant in the believer.

    D. The Holy Spirit ministers to the spirit of the new believer.

2. **If anyone is in Christ, he is a new creation (2 Corinthians 5:17).**

    A. The phrase, "in Christ," refers to our redemptive position in Jesus.

    B. The person who is "in Christ" is said to be born of God, or born again (from above) of the Holy Spirit.

    C. Adam's seed gave birth to living souls, driven by natural propensities; Christ seed gives birth to spiritual beings (1 Corinthians 15:45), controlled by God's life and love in their spirit.

    D. Because we are "in Christ," all that He is and has done are already ours; and in Him we are perfect and complete.

    E. The person who is in Christ shares one spirit with Him.

3. **Our new identity is in Christ, not in Adam.**

    A. What we receive at regeneration (conversion) is real life in our spirit, and not a theological idea or some new intellectual understanding.

    B. The first Adam gave birth to soul children or natural life; the last Adam, Christ, gave birth to spirit children or spiritual life.

    C. The born-again believer has a completely new spiritual identity in Christ.

    D. Satan seeks every opportunity to deceive the child of God into believing that his true identity is his natural physical self—also called "flesh."

    E. The natural or flesh life manifests itself in unrighteousness or self-righteousness.

    F. Self hides at the center of all fleshly behavior.

4. **The eternal Word of God gave birth to the incorruptible seed of the believer's spirit.**

    A. The new man of the believer's incorruptible spirit is a Word product, just like the last Adam, Christ, who fathered him.

    B. When Christ gained the victories over Satan, sin, death and the grave, the incorruptible seed of His spiritual generations was still within Him.

    C. Christ's resurrection gave birth and legitimacy to his bride—the church of the born-again.

    D. The incorruptible seed of Christ's spirit within the believer brings eternal life to the child of God the very instant He receives Jesus as his Savior and Lord.

    E. The believer's new spirit-man cannot sin because he is born of God, and the incorruptible seed of Christ's victorious life reigns within him.

5. **Christ, the last Adam, is the supreme example of what the new spiritual man ought to be.**

A. Christ was, and is, the epitome of what God's "ultimate makeover" of fallen man ought to be.

B. Everything Christ did reflected what everyone, who possesses the incorruptible seed of His life, is able to do.

C. All believers will experience their personal wilderness of temptation, Gethsemane and Calvary in their pilgrimage through this world.

D. Faith in the infallible Word of God is our only defense against the temptations of the devil.

E. All the enemy's temptations are directed at our flesh and natural senses, not our inner spirit-man.

F. We will defeat the enemy whenever we choose to live by the inner man of our spirit.

6. My true identity is not man/woman I see in the mirror.

A. My identity is bound to the identity of Jesus.

B. I am in Christ, He is in me, and we are in the Father (John 14:20).

C. My life should reflect what Jesus would do were He in my place.

D. My identity in Christ is my only hope for victorious living in this life, and my only guarantee for future life in the world to come.

E. The Father, my Savior and I are one.

F. I am God's ultimate makeover—the spiritual edition.

WHO AM I, REALLY?

I AM A NEW CREATION IN CHRIST, A BORN AGAIN SPIRIT-BEING, BORN OF INCORRUPTIBLE SEED THROUGH THE POWER OF THE HOLY SPIRIT WHO OPERATES IN ME. I LIVE IN MY SAVIOR, AND MY SAVIOR LIVES IN ME. THE FATHER ALSO LIVES IN JESUS; WE ARE A PERFECT UNITY. I AM MOST CERTAINLY A KINGDOM CITIZEN, WHOSE LIFE IS FROM ABOVE AND NOT FROM BELOW. I AM INVINCIBLE, UNSTOPPABLE, AND IMMOVABLE, BECAUSE I WALK IN THE AUTHORITY OF MY EXALTED SAVIOR. I SUFFER NO LACK; I HAVE EVERYTHING I NEED; FOR ALL THINGS BELONG TO ME SINCE MY LORD AND I ARE ONE. I AM GOD'S ***ULTIMATE MAKEOVER: THE SPIRITUAL EDITION***.

ULTIMATE MAKEOVER: THE SPIRITUAL EDITION

Lesson 2 – Leader's Notes

1. God is the ultimate Artist, who regenerates or infuses man's depraved spirit with new divine life. This is God's free gift to anyone who receives Jesus as Savior and Lord. The Holy Spirit takes up His abode in man's renewed spirit (inner man) and bears active witness to it. See Ezekiel 36:26, 27; Hebrews 8:10-12; Romans 8:16.

2. If anyone is "in Christ," he is not only a new creation, but is also a part of God's new humanity destined for the new heavens and the new earth which are yet future. "In Christ" points to man's secure, redemptive position in Christ's incorruptible seed. All mankind, including Adam, existed in Christ before the foundation of the world, but this redemptive position does not become viable until a person receives Christ as his Savior. Only then is that person said to be born of God (John 1:12, 13). Unlike our existence through Adam, which is natural, our existence in Christ is totally spiritual (1 Corinthians 15:45). Because we are "in Christ," we share not only His spirit, but His very life (1 Corinthians 6:17)—all that He ever did and taught.

3. Our true identity is no longer in our Adamic nature (2 Corinthians 5:16), but in our spiritual nature in Christ. This existence is not just a theological idea, but a real spirit life in a fleshly body. The devil seeks to divorce us from our true identity in Christ, and have us concentrate all our effort and resources on the outer man of our flesh.

4. We are born again from incorruptible stock, by the Word of God which lives and abides forever (1 Peter 1:23). This incorruptible seed of Christ's life in the believer's spirit brings with itself eternal life instantaneously. Moreover, because this new life originates from God, it cannot commit sin, because the power of Christ's seed life remains within and he cannot sin (1 John 3:9).

5. As the last Adam and head of the new human race, Christ remains our supreme example of what every professed child of God ought to be. Christ stripped His flesh of it power by taking it to the wilderness of testing. In the same way, every child of God must arm himself to face testing and trials (1

Peter 2:21, 22; 4:1, 2) to discipline his flesh to obey the will of God from the heart (or inner spirit-man). The enemy of our souls aims his evil arsenal at our fleshly mind and senses. Active, steadfast faith in the infallible Word of God is our only hope for victory against him and his demonic forces.

6. My true identity is not defined by the man/woman I see in the mirror, but by my spirit life which I share with Christ (1 Corinthians 6:17). Because of this oneness of spirit, my life should be a reflection of what Jesus would live were He in my place. This is my only hope for victory over sin in this life, and my only guarantee for life eternal when my Savior returns. Intrinsically, the Father, my Savior and I are one (John 14:20).

ULTIMATE MAKEOVER: THE SPIRITUAL EDITION

Lesson 2 – Review Questions

1. What is God's primary solution to mankind's identity crisis?

   _____

   _____

2. What does the phrase "in Christ" really mean?

   _____

   _____

3. How does a person become "in Christ"?

   _____

   _____

4. What does being born again really mean?

   _____

   _____

5. What unchangeable creative law characterizes all procreation?

   _____

   _____

6. How does the law of procreation relate to the birth of man's spirit?

   _____

   _____

7. What fundamental truth about his identity every born-again believer needs to clearly understand?

   _____

   _____

   _____

8. What are some of the benefits of the incorruptible seed of the believer's spirit-man?

   _____

   _____

   _____

9. What does the term "flesh" mean?

   _____

   _____

10. What hidden master does "flesh" serve? **Hint:** Turn the word "flesh" backwards.

    _____

11. Why is it necessary for "flesh" to be taken to the wilderness of testing and trial?

12. How should the born-again believer handle temptation?

13. Describe the relationship of the identity of the believer to the identity of Christ and that of the Father.

14. Who are you, really?

ULTIMATE MAKEOVER: THE SPIRITUAL EDITION

Lesson 2 – Answer Key

1. The new creation of his inner spirit-life

2. To share Christ's incorruptible spirit-seed life. Just like to be in Adam mean to share his corruptible flesh-seed life. See **1 Corinthians 6:17; Romans 8:9.**

3. By inviting Jesus to be Savior and Lord of his life; and by being baptized in the name of the Trinity.

4. To receive the incorruptible life of Jesus in one's spirit.

5. Every seed produces after its kind.

6. God is Spirit-life. Therefore everyone who is born of Him is also spirit-life.

7. He is no longer a corruptible fleshly soul but an incorruptible living spirit.

8. It is incorruptible (**1 Peter 1:23**). It cannot sin; it cannot die. See **1 John 3:9; 1 John 5:11, 12.**

9. Self-willed, self-driven. Anything that originates from the natural self—thought, word or deed.

10. Self

11. To strip flesh of its cravings and its power.

12. Believe and confess the Word. Daily focus on feeding his spirit.

13. The identity of the Father, Christ and the believer are ONE (**John 14:20**). The believer must reflect the character of Christ and the Father.

14. A born-again spiritual being. I am divinely human because I carry God's incorruptible life in my spirit.

ULTIMATE MAKEOVER: THE SPIRITUAL EDITION

Lesson 2 – Important Scriptures

"Therefore, if anyone is in Christ, he is a new creation; the old has gone, the new has come!"
2 Corinthians 5:17, NIV

"Moreover, I will give you a new heart and put <u>a new spirit within you</u>; and I will remove the heart of stone from your flesh and give you a heart of flesh. ²⁷I will put <u>My Spirit within you</u> and cause you to walk in My statutes, and you will be careful to observe My ordinances."
Ezekiel 36:26, 27

"FOR THIS IS THE COVENANT THAT I WILL MAKE WITH THE HOUSE OF ISRAEL AFTER THOSE DAYS, SAYS THE LORD: I WILL PUT MY LAWS INTO THEIR MINDS, AND I WILL WRITE THEM ON THEIR HEARTS. AND I WILL BE THEIR GOD, AND THEY SHALL BE MY PEOPLE. ¹¹AND <u>THEY SHALL NOT TEACH EVERYONE HIS FELLOW CITIZEN, AND EVERYONE HIS BROTHER, SAYING, 'KNOW THE LORD,' FOR ALL WILL KNOW ME, FROM THE LEAST TO THE GREATEST OF THEM.</u> ¹²FOR I WILL BE MERCIFUL TO THEIR INIQUITIES, AND I WILL REMEMBER THEIR SINS NO MORE."
Hebrews 8:10-12, NASB

"as many as receive Him, to them He gave the right to become children of God, even to those who believe in His name, <u>who were born</u>, <u>not of blood</u> <u>nor of the will of the flesh</u> <u>nor of the will of man</u>, <u>but of God</u>.
John 1:12, 13

³"Very truly, I tell you, <u>no one can see the kingdom of God without being born from above</u> . . . ⁶Very truly, I tell you, no one can enter the kingdom of God without being <u>born of water and Spirit</u>. What is born of flesh is flesh, <u>what is born of Spirit is spirit</u>."
John 3:3, 6, NRSV

⁴⁵So also it is written, "The first MAN, Adam, BECAME A LIVING SOUL." The last Adam became a life-giving spirit. ⁴⁶However, the spiritual is not first, but the natural; then the spiritual. ⁴⁷The first man is from the earth, earthy; the second man is from heaven. ⁴⁸As is the earthy, so also are those who are earthy; and as is the heavenly, so also are those who are heavenly. ⁴⁹Just as we have borne the image of the earthy, we will also bear the image of the heavenly.

1 Corinthians 15:45-49

"Being born again, not of corruptible seed, but of incorruptible, by the word of God, which liveth and abideth forever."

1 Peter 1:23

¹¹"God has given us eternal life, and <u>this life is in his Son</u>. ¹²<u>He who has the Son has life</u>; he who does not have the Son of God does not have life. ¹³I write these things to <u>you who believe</u> in the name of the Son of God so <u>that you may know that you have eternal life</u>."

1 John 5:11-13

"No one who is born of God practices sin, <u>because His seed abides in him; and he cannot sin</u>, because he is born of God."

1 John 3:9

". . . having concluded this, that <u>one died for all, therefore all died</u>; ¹⁵and He died for all, so that they who live <u>might no longer live for themselves</u>, but for Him who died and rose again on their behalf. ¹⁶<u>Therefore from now on we recognize no one according to the flesh</u>;

2 Corinthians 5:14-16

²¹For you have been called for this purpose, since Christ also suffered for you, leaving you an example for you to follow in His steps, ²²WHO COMMITTED NO SIN, NOR WAS ANY DECEIT FOUND IN HIS MOUTH; ²³and while being reviled, He did not revile in return; while suffering, He uttered no threats, but kept entrusting Himself to Him who judges righteously.

1 Peter 2:21-23

¹Therefore, since Christ has suffered in the flesh, arm yourselves also with the same purpose, because he who has suffered in the flesh has ceased from sin, ²so as to live the rest of the time in the flesh no longer for the lusts of men, but for the will of God.

1 Peter 4:1, 2

But the one who joins himself to the Lord is one spirit with Him.

1 Corinthians 6:17

²⁰"On that day you will realize that <u>I am in my Father</u>, and <u>you are in me</u>, and <u>I am in you</u> . . . ²³If anyone loves me, he will obey my teaching. My Father will love him, and <u>we [the Father and I] will come to him and make our home with him</u>."

John 14:20, 23

DESIGNED FOR SUCCESS

Chapter 3 – Outline

*His divine power has given us **everything we need** for <u>life</u> and <u>godliness</u> through our knowledge of him who called us by his own glory and goodness.*

2 Peter 1:3, NIV, emphasis mine

1. **Seed life is everything for the child of God.**

    *His divine power has given us **everything we need** for <u>life</u> and <u>godliness</u> through our knowledge of him who called us by his own glory and goodness* (2 Peter 1:3).

    A. The incorruptible seed of our inner spirit life comes fully equipped with everything we need for life and godlikeness.

    B. Whether they perceive this or not, all born-again believers share this one thing in common with one another—that is, the Spirit of the life of God within themselves.

    C. The inner spirit-man of the born-again believer shares in the divine nature of the life of God.

    D. Therefore, the incorruptible seed of the believer's spirit comes pre-packaged to succeed.

2. **The corruptible seed of our Adam life (flesh) must die in order for the incorruptible seed of Christ life (spirit) to live and reign within us.**

    A. Unless a seed is planted in the earth and dies, it will not germinate and bear fruit.

    B. Jesus was God's incorruptible Seed that came to the earth to die and give resurrected life to all who believe in Him.

C. We too must yield up the life of our fleshly soul so that the seed of Christ spirit-life may germinate and bear fruit to the glory of God.

D. It is the "hating" (denying) of self that leads to the dying of self and the growing of spirit.

3. **Through His resurrected life, Christ has released a spirit of faith and freedom in every believer.**

    A. The inner man in every child of God is a spirit of freedom and faith, not of bondage and fear.

    B. The born-again individual does not need to work on his flesh to obey; obedience is already enshrined in the inner man of his spirit.

    C. Therefore, the spiritual man is not bound by Law, for the life of Christ in his spirit has set him free from the Law of sin and death.

    D. Freedom of one's spirit is not a license for breaking God's Law.

    E. It is totally impossible for the man of the flesh to do spiritual work, and equally impossible for the spirit-man to do fleshly work.

    F. The key to maintaining our freedom in Christ is to live our lives every day from the impregnable platform of our true spiritual identity.

4. **Because of Christ's super-abounding victory over Satan, sin, death and the grave, He has given a birth to an incorruptible, dominion seed in every believer.**

    A. Man was created to have dominion—not to be dominated—but he lost it after the fall.

    B. Seed is most important commodity in the salvation-history of the human race.

    C. The seed of the serpent (devil) was sown in human nature (flesh); the seed of the woman (Jesus) is deposited in the believer's renewed spirit.

D. Only the seed of the Spirit can wage war successfully against the seed of the flesh.

E. The dominion Seed of God took our nature so that, through His death, He could render powerless the seed of the devil in our nature.

F. The resurrection of Christ was a resurrection of God's dominion Seed; and we are its harvest.

5. **We have dominion over our flesh and sin by living from the invincible platform of our inner spirit-man.**

   A. There is absolutely no sin in our flesh that cannot be broken by the dominion Seed of the woman (Jesus) operating in our inner man through the power of the Holy Spirit.

   B. The only way to victory over sin in our flesh is through the dominion seed of our inner spirit-man.

   C. Faith that produces the works of God can only come when the spirit-filled words of God, connect with the Spirit-generated spirit-man in the believer.

   D. There is a spiritual disconnection between our faith and our works because we try to appropriate these elements through the wrong man—that is, the man of our flesh, instead of the inner man of the spirit.

   E. Sin shall not have dominion over us because we are the harvest of the dominion Seed of the woman.

DESIGNED FOR SUCCESS

Lesson 3 – Leader's Notes

1. Incorruptible seed life is everything to the child of God, because this inner life in his spirit comes fully equipped with everything that pertains to life and godliness (2 Peter 1:3). The nature of this seed-life is not human but divine (verse 4), because it was created in righteous and holy nature of God (Ephesians 4:24). Therefore, the believer's new nature comes pre-packaged for success pre-ordained by God, Himself (Ephesians 2:10).

2. We must be willing and ready to put to death daily (via self-denial), the corruptible seed life we have inherited through Adam, in order for the incorruptible seed of Christ's life to live and reign within us. Just as a seed must die in order to germinate and bear fruit, we must consistently deny the desire of our fleshly soul so that Christ's seed in us may germinate and bear fruit to His glory.

3. Through His resurrected life, Christ has released a spirit of faith and freedom, not fear and bondage, to every believer. Therefore, the believer does not need to work on his flesh in order to obey the requirements of Law. Obedience to Law is already enshrined in the inner man of his spirit. In that sense, the inner spirit man is not governed by Law, but by the power of the Life that fulfilled (or met) all the requirements of Law (Romans 8:1-4). Just as it is utterly impossible for the natural man to do spiritual work, it is equally impossible for the spiritual man to do fleshly work.

4. Christ's super-abounding victory over Satan, sin, death and the grave operates in the DNA of the incorruptible, dominion seed in the spirit of every believer. The sad truth is that most believers do not know or understand this marvelous faith transaction provided by God's grace and mercy. While the seed of the serpent was sown in human nature (flesh), the seed of the woman (Jesus) is deposited in the believer's renewed spirit. The seed of the woman took our nature so that through His death He could destroy the seed of the devil in our nature (1 John 3:8).

5. We can have dominion over our fleshly craving and sin only by living our lives from the invincible platform of our inner spirit-man, for there is

absolutely no sin or weakness in our flesh that cannot be broken by the victorious, resurrected life of Jesus operating in us. Sin cannot have dominion over us if allow the Christ in our spirit—not the "I" in our flesh—to live and reign (Romans 6:14; Galatians 2:20; 5:16). We often fail in our battle with sin and weakness because we try to achieve victory through the natural powers of our Adam-man, instead of our Christ-man on the inside. This is impossible, and can be likened to using Satan to fight sin. See Romans 8:5-14.

DESIGNED FOR SUCCESS

Lesson 3 – Review Questions

1. What invaluable spiritual element do all believers share with one another?

   _____

   _____

2. What makes the incorruptible seed of man's renewed spirit God's guarantee for restoring fallen man in His image again?

   _____

   _____

3. How does the death of our Adamic self (flesh) relate to the life and function of the incorruptible seed of our spirit-man?

   _____

   _____

   _____

4. In what sense is the believer born-again to freedom?

   _____

   _____

   _____

5. What is the key to maintaining one's freedom in Christ and living a life of victory over sin?

_____

_____

6. What is God's "rule of engagement" in the great controversy between good and evil?

_____

_____

7. What is the seed of the woman?

_____

_____

8. What is the seed of the serpent?

_____

_____

9. How does Christ's dominion over the seed of the serpent (fallen human nature/flesh) relate to the believer's battle against sin and evil?

_____

_____

10. What two forces battle for the control of the believer' mind?

_____

11. Complete the sentence: *The incorruptible seed of the believer's spirit has been designed for . . .*

_____

_____

DESIGNED FOR SUCCESS

Lesson 3 – Answer Key

1. The Spirit of the life of God.

2. It contains the divine gene (Christ's DNA) to produce the life of God in the believer. See **2 Peter 1:4, Ephesians 4:24**.

3. The flesh seed of Adam must die in order that the spirit seed of Christ might live.

4. He is not bound by the law of sin and death that once held sway over his fleshly (sinful) soul. See **Romans 8:2.**

5. To live our lives every day from the impregnable platform of our true spiritual identity.

6. The seed of the woman and the seed of the serpent will fight against each other till the end of time.

7. Christ's incorruptible spirit.

8. Adam's corrupt flesh.

9. Christ's dominion over sin already resides in His incorruptible seed-life within the spirit of the believer. Once the believer focuses all his attention on the nurture and growth of his seed life, victory over sin is guaranteed.

10. The Seed of the woman (spirit-seed) and the seed of the serpent (flesh-seed).

11. Freedom, dominion and success.

DESIGNED FOR SUCCESS

Lesson 3 – Important Scriptures

*His divine power has given us **everything we need** for life and godliness through our knowledge of him who called us by his own glory and goodness.*
2 Peter 1:3, NIV, emphasis mine

And that ye put on the new man, which after God is created in righteousness and true holiness.
Ephesians 4:24

[10]For we are His workmanship, created in Christ Jesus for good works, which God prepared beforehand so that we would walk in them.
Ephesians 2:10

"For you have not received a spirit of slavery leading to fear again, but you have received a spirit of adoption as sons by which we cry out, 'Abba! Father!'"
Romans 8:15

[1]"Therefore there is now no condemnation for those who are in Christ Jesus. [2]For the law of the Spirit of life in Christ Jesus has set you free from the law of sin and of death. [3]For what the Law could not do, weak as it was through the flesh, God did: sending His own Son in the likeness of sinful flesh and as an offering for sin, He condemned sin in the flesh, [4]so that the requirement of the Law might be fulfilled in us, who do not walk according to the flesh but according to the Spirit."
Romans 8:1-4

"But now that you have been set free from sin and have become slaves to God, the benefit you reap leads to holiness, and the result is eternal life. [23]For the wages of sin is death, but the gift of God is eternal life in Christ Jesus our Lord."
Romans 6:22, 23, NIV

The one who practices sin is of the devil; for the devil has sinned from the beginning. The Son of God appeared for this purpose, to destroy the works of the devil.

1John 3:8

"For sin shall not have dominion over you: for ye are not under the law, but under grace."

Romans 6:14, KJV

"Stand fast therefore in the liberty wherewith Christ hath made us free, and be not entangled again with the yoke of bondage."

Galatians 5:1, KJV

"I have been crucified with Christ; and it is no longer I who live, but Christ lives in me; and the life which I now live in the flesh I live by faith in the Son of God, who loved me and gave Himself up for me."

Galatians 2:20

But I say, walk by the Spirit, and you will not carry out the desire of the flesh.

Galatians 5:16.

BRIDGING THE GAP

Chapter 4 – Outline

. . . the one who says he abides in Him ought himself to walk in the same manner as He walked.

1 John 2:6

1. **How do believers connect with the new creation of Christ's incorruptible spirit-seed within themselves?**

   A. There is a prevailing breach between what the born-again believer professes to be and what he actually lives.

   B. Many believers fail to launch their Christian experience because they lack the full understanding of what it means to be born again.

   C. Some of God's children experience "arrested spiritual development" because they fail to recognize God's new creation of their inner spiritual life that was born of the Holy Spirit.

2. **Every believer needs to be introduced to his new life in the spiritual realm.**

   A. The incorruptible seed-life of the born-again believer is a spiritual baby which bears the imprint of the Savior.

   B. That baby needs to be nourished by the pure "milk" of the Word of God and nurtured by spiritual discipline—meditation, prayer, fasting, etc.

   C. Many professed Christians are guilty of child neglect and spiritual abuse.

   D. These individuals may be intellectually and physically strong, but woefully lacking in faith and spiritual maturity.

   E. It is very important for every believer to develop spirit-consciousness in order to interact daily with his new inner life.

3. **Since the child of God is born from above, he/she must be taught how to think and act in concert with life from his/her homeland—heaven.**

    A. This involves learning anew how to hear, see, speak and walk by his spirit-life from above.

    B. The ways of being and knowing in the natural realm are vastly different from the ways of being and knowing in the spiritual realm.

    C. The natural man uses the avenues of his five senses to perceive and interact with his environment.

    D. The spiritual man is driven by the organs of his intuition, conscience and communion, which receive instruction from the Holy Spirit and the Word of God.

    E. The Child of God must allow the demands of his inner life to rule over everything driven by his natural or soul life.

    F. The Word of God alone, is the authoritative judge that decides whether a thought, word or action is arising from the spirit or the soul (flesh) of the believer.

4. **The tree of the knowledge of good and evil feeds the wisdom of man and the systems of the world.**

    A. God gave specific instructions regarding the tree of the knowledge of good and evil.

    B. Obey and live forever; disobey and you will surely die.

    C. The tree of the knowledge of good and evil represented a life totally independent of God—one that was self-willed, self-propelled and self-directed.

    D. The fruits of the tree of knowledge of good and evil personified the evil ambition of the deceptive serpent, Satan—to be like the Most High God (Isaiah 14:12-14).

E. The wisdom of man, which drives the systems of the world, is fed from the tree of the knowledge of good and evil.

F. All who feed from that tree are overtaken by the same proud, ambitious, selfish spirit of the evil one.

G. God stands in opposition to the wisdom of this world because it is driven by the tree of the knowledge of good and evil, whose planter is the evil one.

5. **The tree of Life and the tree of the knowledge of good and evil represent two diametrically opposite lifestyles in this world.**

    A. The tree of Life feeds and supports spirit-life, which lives and operates through utter dependence on EVERY word of God.

    B. The tree of the knowledge of good and evil feeds and supports flesh or soul life, which lives and operates through utter dependence on self.

    C. The tree of Life produces a lifestyle that is filled with the fruit of the Spirit.

    D. The tree of the knowledge produces a lifestyle that is filled with the fruits of the flesh.

    E. Those who feed from the tree of Life are driven by faith; those who survive by feeding on the tree of the knowledge of good and evil are driven by fear.

6. **The Holy Spirit is the Divine Transformer who bridges the gap between the believer's position in Christ and experience in Christ; and between his profession of Christ and performance in Christ.**

    A. The role of the Holy Spirit is to train and facilitate the growth of the incorruptible seed into the stature and fullness of the One who created him.

    B. Pentecost transformed the once fearful, self-centered followers of Christ into fearless, contagious disciples of the kingdom.

C. The latter rain—the next Pentecost for last-day believers—would bring about the same transformation, but an exceedingly more glorious harvest of souls for the kingdom of God.

D. Every disciple who is actively engaged in seeking the salvation of the lost will be anointed by the Holy Spirit during the period just prior to the end of the world and the return of Jesus.

E. Serving God aright begins with the inner spirit-man (heart), which governs the soul (mind, emotions and will) to direct the body in the ways of God.

F. The seed of the serpent is sown in our soul and body, and these organs are powerless against all the attacks of the enemy.

BRIDGING THE GAP

Lesson 4 – Leader's Notes

1. There is a prevailing disconnection between what the born-again believer professes to be and what he actually lives. This is due primarily to spiritual ignorance and misunderstanding of what it means to be born again. Consequently, many of God's children experience "arrested spiritual development" (ASD) because they fail to recognize and connect with God's new creation of their inner spiritual life that was born of the Holy Spirit. Therefore, their spirit-man is neglected and his growth is stunted.

2. Every believer needs to be introduced to his new inner life—the incorruptible seed of his spirit-man. He must know that his life is indeed a spiritual infant—just as real as his natural existence. This new creation bears the perfect, sinless imprint of the Savior, and must be nourished by the pure milk of the Word and nurtured through spiritual discipline—meditation on the Word, prayer, fasting, worship, acts of benevolence, etc. Sadly, though, many professed Christians lack spirit-consciousness, and, therefore, spend most of their waking hours facilitating the needs of their natural flesh life than catering to the needs of their inner spirit-life.

3. Since the believer's new life is from above—that, from God, Himself—he must be taught how to think and live in harmony with life that pertains to his true homeland—heaven (Colossians 3:1, 2; Philippians 3:20). He must learn new ways of being and knowing that are foreign to natural life and reasoning ability. Through the organ of his inner spirit-man, he must develop new ways of hearing, seeing, speaking and walking (or conduct) that reflect life from his heavenly home. In this regard, the Word of God, which is the spiritual mother of his new life (1 Peter 1:23), is the divine instrument, apart from the Holy Spirit, for maintaining the life and growth of the believer's spirit (Matthew 4:4; 1 Peter 2:2; Proverbs 4:20-22).

4. The tree of the knowledge of good and evil feeds the wisdom of man and the systems that run the course of the world. Its nourishment sustains the form of life that is self-willed, self-propelled and self-directed, and that life is characterized by the same proud, ambitious spirit of the evil one who planted it. God stands in opposition to the wisdom of this world because it

is driven by the tree of the knowledge of good and evil that fuels the selfish, rebellious spirit of the evil one in mankind.

5. The tree of life and the tree of the knowledge of good and evil represent two diametrically opposite lifestyle, one that operates through utter dependence on EVERY word of God, and the other that functions by depending on self. One lifestyle is driven by faith, the other is driven by fear; one produces the fruit of the spirit, the other yields the deeds of the flesh.

6. The Holy Spirit is the Divine Transformer who bridges the gap between the believer's position in Christ and his daily experience in Christ; and between his profession of Christ and performance in Christ. Serving God aright always begins with the inner man of the believer's spirit and not the outer man of his flesh. It is the divine connection of the Spirit of God with the spirit in man (Romans 8:16) that empowers the human soul to obey the perfect will of God. The latter rain (Zechariah 10:1; Joel 2:28, 29) will mature the incorruptible seed of Christ in the believer's spirit, empowering all His last-day disciples to prepare earth's harvest for the Lord's return.

BRIDGING THE GAP

Lesson 4 – Review Questions

1. Explain what is described in this volume as "arrested spiritual development" (ASD)?

   _____

   _____

2. What spiritual ignorance accounts for this very prevalent and tragic phenomenon (ASD) among professed believers?

   _____

   _____

3. What should be the very first work of those responsible for discipling new believers in Christ?

   _____

   _____

4. Why does it become necessary for the born-again believer to develop a new sense of being, learning and knowing in order to live the victorious life of faith in Jesus?

   _____

   _____

5. What must the child of God develop in order to be aware of his inner life and spiritual environment?

   _____

   _____

6. Why it is that natural intelligence cannot comprehend the things delivered by the Spirit of God?

   _____

   _____

7. What two infallible authorities hold sway over the mind of the believer's spirit-man?

   _____

8. What deceptive source feeds the wisdom of this world?

   _____

9. The mind of the natural man is driven by fear; the mind of the inner spirit-man is driven by

   _____

10. The foundation of fear is human reason; the foundation of faith is

    _____

    _____

11. Who is the divine Transformer?

   _____

12. What is the greatest work given to the church?

   _____

   _____

13. Man's approach to problem-solving is to begin with mental processing, followed by fleshly action; the Spirit's way is to begin with

   _____

   _____

14. The believer's inner spirit-man is his spiritual GPS. What is the meaning of this acronym?

   _____

   _____

BRIDGING THE GAP

Lesson 4 – Answer Key

1. The failure of their inner spirit-man to grow and mature into the image of the One who created him—that is Christ.

2. Ignorance of their true identity in Christ—the incorruptible seed of their inner spirit-man.

3. Teach new believers how to connect with and nurture their inner spirit life in Christ.

4. Because his new inner spirit life does not function by the norms of his old, natural self.

5. Spirit-consciousness.

6. Because they can only be appraised by man's spirit, not his fleshly mind. See **1 Corinthians 2:14.**

7. The Holy Spirit and the holy Word of God.

8. The tree of the knowledge of good and evil.

9. Faith.

10. God and His infallible Word.

11. The Holy Spirit.

12. To find the lost and to teach believers how to become imitators of their Master.

13. Waiting and listening in the presence of the Great I AM, in spite of the urgings of our fleshly mind to do otherwise.

14. God-directed Positioning System. See **Proverb 20:27.**

BRIDGING THE GAP

Lesson 4 – Important Scriptures

. . . the one who says he abides in Him ought himself to walk in the same manner as He walked.
1 John 2:6

So then, just as you received Christ Jesus as Lord, continue to live in him.
Colossians 2:6, NIV

"Can a woman forget her nursing child and have no compassion on the son of her womb? Even these may forget . . ."
Isaiah 49:15

My people are destroyed for lack of knowledge . . .
Hosea 4:6

⁴My message and my preaching were not with wise and persuasive words, but with a demonstration of the Spirit's power, ⁵so that your faith might not rest on <u>men's wisdom</u>, but on <u>God's power</u>. ⁶We do, however, speak <u>a message of wisdom among the mature</u>, but not <u>the wisdom of this age</u> or of the rulers of this age, who are coming to nothing. ⁷No, we speak of <u>God's secret wisdom</u>, a <u>wisdom that has been hidden</u> and <u>that God destined for our glory before time began</u>.
1 Corinthians 2:4-7, NIV

"For My thoughts are not your thoughts, nor are your ways My ways," declares the LORD. ⁹"For as the heavens are higher than the earth, so are My ways higher than your ways And My thoughts than your thoughts."
Isaiah 55:8, 9

¹⁷That the God of our Lord Jesus Christ, the Father of glory, may give unto you <u>the spirit of wisdom and revelation in the knowledge of him</u>: ¹⁸The <u>eyes of your

understanding being enlightened; that ye may know what is the hope of his calling, and what the riches of the glory of his inheritance in the saints,
Ephesians 1:17, 18

For the word of God is living and active and sharper than any two-edged sword, and piercing as far as the division of soul and spirit, of both joints and marrow, and able to judge the thoughts and intentions of the heart.
Hebrews 4:12

⁸The LORD God planted a garden toward the east, in Eden; and there He placed the man whom He had formed. ⁹Out of the ground the LORD God caused to grow every tree that is pleasing to the sight and good for food; the tree of life also in the midst of the garden, and the tree of the knowledge of good and evil.
Genesis 2:8, 9

¹⁶The LORD God commanded the man, saying, "From any tree of the garden you may eat freely; ¹⁷but from the tree of the knowledge of good and evil you shall not eat, for in the day that you eat from it you will surely die."
Genesis 2:16, 17

"You surely will not die! ⁵For God knows that in the day you eat from it your eyes will be opened, and you will be like God, knowing good and evil."
Genesis 3:4, 5

"I WILL DESTROY THE WISDOM OF THE WISE, AND THE CLEVERNESS OF THE CLEVER I WILL SET ASIDE." ²⁰Where is the wise man? Where is the scribe? Where is the debater of this age? Has not God made foolish the wisdom of the world? . . . ²⁵ Because the foolishness of God is wiser than men, and the weakness of God is stronger than men . . . ²⁷but God has chosen the foolish things of the world to shame the wise, and God has chosen the weak things of the world to shame the things which are strong, ²⁸and the base things of the world and the despised God has chosen, the things that are not, so that He may nullify the things that are, ²⁹so that no man may boast before God.
1 Corinthians 1:19-29

. . . live by the Spirit, and you will not gratify the desires of the sinful nature.
Galatians 5:16, NIV

But the anointing which ye have received of him abideth in you, and ye need not that any man teach you: but as the same anointing teacheth you of all things, and is truth, and is no lie, and even as it hath taught you, ye shall abide in him.
1 John 2:27, KJV

Therefore, if anyone is in Christ, he is a new creation; the old has gone, the new has come! ¹⁸All this is from God, <u>who reconciled us to himself</u> through Christ <u>and gave us the ministry of reconciliation</u>: ¹⁹that God was reconciling the world to himself in Christ, not counting men's sins against them. And <u>he has committed to us the message of reconciliation</u>. ²⁰<u>We are therefore Christ's ambassadors</u>, as though God were making his appeal through us. We implore you on Christ's behalf: Be reconciled to God.
2 Corinthians 5:17-20, NIV

²³So rejoice, O sons of Zion, And be glad in the LORD your God; For He has given you the early rain for your vindication. And He has poured down for you the rain, The early and latter rain as before. ²⁴The threshing floors will be full of grain, And the vats will overflow with the new wine and oil. . . ²⁷Thus you will know that I am in the midst of Israel, And that I am the LORD your God, And there is no other; And My people will never be put to shame. ²⁸It will come about after this That I will pour out My Spirit on all mankind; And your sons and daughters will prophesy, Your old men will dream dreams, Your young men will see visions. ²⁹Even on the male and female servants I will pour out My Spirit in those days.
Joel 2:23-29

"Ask ye of the LORD rain in the time of the latter rain; so the LORD shall make bright clouds, and give them showers of rain, to every ONE grass in the field."
Zechariah 10:1

And the very God of peace sanctify you wholly; and I pray God your <u>whole spirit</u> and <u>soul</u> and <u>body</u> be preserved blameless unto the coming of our Lord Jesus Christ.
1 Thessalonians 5:23

Trust in the LORD with <u>all thine heart</u>; and lean not unto thine own understanding. In <u>all thy ways</u> acknowledge him, and he shall direct thy paths. Be not wise in thine own eyes:

Proverbs 3:5-7, KJV

[9]However, as it is written: "No eye has seen, no ear has heard, no mind has conceived what God has prepared for those who love him"— [10]<u>but God has revealed it to us by his Spirit</u>. The Spirit searches <u>all things</u>, <u>even the deep things of God</u>. [11]For who among men knows the thoughts of a man except the man's spirit within him? In the same way <u>no one knows the thoughts of God except the Spirit of God</u>. [12]<u>We have</u> not received the spirit of the world but <u>the Spirit who is from God</u>, <u>that we may understand</u> <u>what God has freely given us</u>.

1 Corinthians 2:9-12

PART II

TRAINING YOUR SPIRIT-MAN

Train yourself in godliness, ⁸for, while physical training is of some value, godliness is valuable in every way, holding promise for both the present life and the life to come.

1 Timothy 4:7, 8, (NRSV)

"*If we live by the Spirit, let us also walk by the Spirit*"

Galatians 5:20

The very first order of business for the believing community, with regard to new converts to the gospel of Jesus, should not be that of indoctrination or community socialization. Although these are important, they should not take precedence over guiding the new believer into connecting with, and into nurturing and training, his inner spirit-man for his kingdom mission and assignment. This is of utmost importance because the success of the convert's entire Christian experience depends on his perfect understanding of who he is in Christ Jesus.

It is from this incorruptible platform of his inner spirit-life, and not from his fleshly soul, that the new believer is able to wage war successfully with the enemy, and grow gracefully into the full stature of the One who gave birth to him—even Jesus Christ. He, Himself, stated that when the disciple is fully trained He will be like his teacher (Luke 6:40).

Paul encouraged young Timothy to train himself (his inner life) in godliness, for such training is profitable, not only for life in this world, but also in the world to come (1 Timothy 4:7, 8). In speaking about his spiritual training to the Christians in Corinth, the veteran apostle said:

Therefore I run in such a way, as not without aim; I box in such a way, as not beating the air; ²⁷but I discipline my body and make it my slave, so that, after I have preached to others, I myself will not be disqualified.

1 Corinthians 9:26, 27

The child of God must be resolute and disciplined with regard to surrendering the powers of his fleshly soul to the control of the inner life of Christ in his spirit.

Like Paul, he should not waste time shadow-boxing with his carnal desires; but must bring his body under strict obedience to the call of his spirit, and make absolutely no provision for his flesh (Romans 13:14).

In this section, we will explore how the inner man of Christ's incorruptible seed is able to train the believer to walk (or live) in the perfect will of God through the influence of the Holy Spirit. It is this living and walking by the Spirit that affords the believer the power to imitate the life of God that was personified in Jesus.

LEARNING TO HEAR AGAIN

Chapter 5 – Outline

¹³For <u>whosoever shall call</u> upon the name of the Lord shall be saved. ¹⁴<u>How then shall they call</u> on him in whom they <u>have not believed</u>? And how shall they believe in him of whom they <u>have not heard</u>? And how shall they <u>hear</u> without a preacher? . . . ¹⁷So then <u>faith cometh by hearing</u>, and <u>hearing by the word of God</u> (Romans 10:13-17).

1. **The Word of God is everything to the spirit-man.**

   A. A "Wordless" Christian—one who does not feed on the Word daily—is a "fleshy" Christian.

   B. There is absolutely no other man-made product or formulation in the world that could stand on the same platform as God's eternal Word.

   C. The most significant receptive faculty for the growth and development of the spirit-man in every believer is the organ of hearing.

   D. Spiritual hearing and natural hearing operate on two different and incompatible frequencies.

   E. The organ of hearing in the spiritual realm is not the physical ear, but the un-erring Word of God and the spirit of man.

   F. The un-regenerated sinner cannot hear to any degree of clarity the thing pertaining to the realm of the Spirit.

2. **Victorious faith involves the diligent training of the spirit-man to hear and receive the Word, more than the educating of the mind about what is in the Word.**

   A. There is a direct line of communication between the Word of God and the regenerated spirit-man.

B. The spirit is designed to obey the demands of the Word of God because they originated from the same Source—God.

C. The incorruptible seed of man's spirit is programmed to short-circuit or by-pass the faculty of reason.

D. A faith-based decision is not influenced by what is fed to the brain from the five senses.

3. The child of God must pay very careful attention to what he allows himself to hear.

A. What we hear and process invariably influences the decisions we make.

B. The words we allow ourselves to hear have the power to influence the course of our lives.

C. Hearing the words of a talebearer has the potential to wreak havoc in a person's life.

D. It is the hearing of, and meditation upon, the Word of God that will yield fruitfulness in the believer's life.

E. The un-erring Word of God is a self-fulfilling prophecy.

4. The child of God must pay very careful attention to HOW he hears.

A. How we hear depends on what we have going on in our spirit (heart) and mind.

B. We must learn how to be still in His presence in order to hear with clarity what God is communicating to us.

C. The real secret to a listening "ear" is a broken and contrite spirit.

D. Our ability to hear God's Word will influence the quality of our judgments regarding all the situations of our lives.

LEARNING TO HEAR AGAIN

Lesson 5 – Leader's Notes

1. The unfailing Word of God is everything to the inner man of the believer's spirit. His every decision and function depends upon his unbroken relationship and response to its precepts and promises. In this regard, the most significant receptive faculty for promoting the growth and development of the spirit-man in every believer, is the sense of hearing. Spiritual hearing operates on a completely different level to natural hearing. The true sense of hearing for the spirit-man is not the natural ears of the physical man, but the un-erring Word of God. Everything that the inner spirit-man hears and receives must pass the Word's uncompromising scrutiny and approval.

2. Victorious faith involves the diligent training of the spirit-man to hear and receive the Word, more than the educating of the mind of the natural man about what is in the Word. Faith comes from hearing the Word of God (Romans 10:17). There is a direct line of communication between the Word of God and the regenerated spirit-man, for he has been pre-programmed to implicitly accept and obey all its teachings. A faith-based decision is not influenced simply by what is fed to the brain through the five senses, but by what the Word of God says regarding the content of the feeding source.

3. Every believer must pay strict attention to what he allows to enter the portals of his ears, because what he allows himself to hear will influence the decisions he makes, the words he speaks and the actions he performs (Mark 4:23, 24). It is the hearing and doing of the Word of God that will yield fruitfulness in the believer's life.

4. The child of God must pay careful attention not only to what he allows himself to hear, but also to process of hearing—that is, how he hears and analyzes the information (Luke 8:18). How one hears depends more on what one has going on in one's spirit and mind than on what passes through one's ears. God's children must learn how to quiet their cluttered minds in His awesome presence so that they could hear with some degree of clarity what He is communicating to them. In the context of spiritual hearing, the secret to a listening "ear" is a broken and contrite spirit.

LEARNING TO HEAR AGAIN

Lesson 5 – Review Questions

1. What type of Christian is a "Wordless" Christian?

   _____

2. Why is it necessary for the believer to learn to hear again?

   _____

   _____

3. What relationship exists between faith and spiritual hearing?

   _____

4. The physical ears are the hearing organs of the natural man; what is the hearing organ of the spirit-man?

   _____

   _____

5. How does the spirit-man hear?

   _____

6. Faith originates from man's intelligence. True or False?

   _____

7. How does a person develop victorious faith?

8. Why it is so very important for a believer to pay very strict attention to what he hears?

9. What power do the words of a talebearer possess?

10. Why is it equally so very important for a believer to pay very close attention to how he hears?

11. What influences how we hear spiritually?

12. What are spirit-ears?

LEARNING TO HEAR AGAIN

Lesson 5 – Answer Key

1. Carnal.

2. Because it is the most significant receptive faculty for the growth and development of the spirit-man in every believer.

3. Faith comes by the ability of the spirit-man to hear the Word of God.

4. The unerring Word of God.

5. By filtering all that the natural ear receives through the Word of God.

6. False. It originates from man's spirit.

7. By training the inner spirit-man to hear and obey the Word.

8. Because what we hear has the potential to affect our speech and the course of our life.

9. Power to poison our innermost being.

10. Because it will determine not only what he hears, but also the decision he makes in regards to what he says and how he lives.

11. The condition of our spirit and mind.

12. Spirit-ears are the inner ears of the soul (spirit-man) which hear all sound only through the Holy Spirit and the Word of God.

LEARNING TO HEAR AGAIN

Lesson 5 – Important Scriptures

^{13}For <u>whosoever shall call</u> upon the name of the Lord shall be saved. ^{14}<u>How then shall they call</u> on him in whom they <u>have not believed</u>? And how shall they believe in him of whom they <u>have not heard</u>? And how shall they <u>hear</u> without a preacher? . . . ^{17}So then <u>faith cometh by hearing</u>, and <u>hearing by the word of God</u>.

Romans 10:13-17

^{13}"Therefore I speak to them in parables; because . . . while <u>hearing they do not hear</u>, nor do they understand. ^{14}In their case the prophecy of Isaiah is being fulfilled, which says, '<u>YOU WILL KEEP ON HEARING, BUT WILL NOT UNDERSTAND</u>; . . . ^{15}FOR HEART OF THIS PEOPLE HAS BECOME DULL, WITH THEIR EARS THEY SCARCELY HEAR, . . . OTHERWISE THEY WOULD. . . HEAR THEIR EARS, AND UNDERSTAND WITH THEIR HEART AND RETURN, AND I WOULD HEAL THEM.' ^{16}But <u>blessed are . . . your ears, because they hear</u>."

Matthew 13:13-16

^{8}But what does it say? "THE WORD IS NEAR YOU, in your mouth and <u>in your heart</u>"—that is, the word of faith which we are preaching, ^{9}that if you confess with your mouth Jesus as Lord, and <u>believe in your heart</u> that God raised Him from the dead, you will be saved; ^{10}for <u>with the heart a person believes</u>, resulting in righteousness, and with the mouth he confesses, resulting in salvation.

Romans 10:8-10

We having the same spirit of faith, according as it is written, I believed, and therefore have I spoken; we also believe, and therefore speak;

2 Corinthians 4:13

If any man has ears to hear, let him hear. ^{24}And he said unto them, Take heed what ye hear: with what measure ye mete, it shall be measured to you: and unto you that hear shall more be given.

Mark 4:23, 24, KJV

My son, <u>give attention to my words</u>; <u>Incline your ear</u> to my sayings. ²¹Do not let them <u>depart from your sight</u>; Keep them <u>in the midst of your heart</u>. ²²For <u>they are life</u> to those who find them and <u>health to all their body</u>. Watch over your heart with all diligence, for from it flow the springs of life.

Proverbs 4:20-23

"But the Helper, the Holy Spirit, whom the Father will send in My name, <u>He will teach you all things</u>, and <u>bring to your remembrance</u> <u>all that I said to you</u>."

John 14:26

As for you, the anointing which you received from Him abides in you, and <u>you have no need for anyone to teach you</u>; but as <u>His anointing teaches you about all things</u>, and is true and is not a lie, and just as it has taught you, you abide in Him.

1 John 2:27

"Therefore consider carefully how you listen. Whoever has will be given more; whoever does not have, even what he thinks he has will be taken from him."

Luke 8:18, NIV

⁴The Lord GOD has given Me the tongue of disciples, that I may know how to sustain the weary one with a word. He awakens Me morning by morning, <u>He awakens My ear to listen as a disciple</u>. ⁵The Lord GOD has opened My ear; And <u>I was not disobedient</u> <u>nor did I turn back</u>.

Isaiah 50:3, 4

By myself I can do nothing; <u>I judge only as I hear</u>, and my judgment is just, for I seek not to please myself but him who sent me.

John 5:30

LEARNING TO SEE AGAIN

Chapter 6 – Outline

"The eye is the lamp of the body. If your eyes are good, your whole body will be full of light. ²³But if your eyes are bad, your whole body will be full of darkness. If then the light within you is darkness, how great is that darkness!" (Matthew 6:22, 23).

1. **The spirit of man can be compared to the eyes of his body.**

    A. The condition of the eyes determine the amount of light the body receives.

    B. The spirit of man provides light, vision and direction to his soul.

    C. The entire body of the carnal man is in deep obscurity because the light from his spirit is really darkness.

    D. The god of this world has shrouded the minds of men with darkness so that they cannot see the light of the gospel of the glory of Christ.

2. **Christ, God's Lamp, gives light to all who come into the world.**

    A. To have the Light of life means to have the life of Christ within you.

    B. Because our spirit abides in this body of death (Romans 7:24), our spiritual vision remains partially impaired until we receive our new body from heaven.

    C. The inner man of the spirit lives in God's light and cannot walk peaceably in the way of darkness.

    D. All who walk in the Light will have fellowship with one another.

    E. Many professing Christianity in the Laodicean church age are walking in darkness while professing to have great light.

3. **Spirit vision does not depend on what the eyes behold.**

    A. While the believer is a born-again spiritual being, he is still confronted and encumbered by his body of death and the cravings of his fleshly existence.

    B. Without enlightenment from the Holy Spirit, it will be totally impossible for even the born-again believer to see through the eyes of his spirit or mind of his soul.

    C. For the believer who chooses to walk by his inner spirit-life, believing is seeing; not the other way around.

4. **The inner man of our spirit sees by adjusting the short-sighted focus of our natural vision to precepts of the Word of God.**

    A. In the natural world, reality is defined by whatever one perceives through the avenues of the five senses. However, in the realm of the spirit, reality is determined, only by what God says.

    B. The eyes of the inner spirit-man are the living Word of God.

    C. The vision of the spirit-man is facilitated by focusing the attention on the things which are not seen, and not on the things that he is momentarily experiencing.

    D. Examples of these things which are not seen are the provision, healing, deliverance, protection, and every other blessing, declaration, and promise that the infallible Word of the God has already proclaimed.

    E. God is the ultimate reality that never changes. He alone can establish what is, or is not, real, by the power of His Word.

    F. We must, therefore, train our soul-man—him who we received from Adam—to see all of life through the eyes of our spirit-man—him who we received from Christ (1 Corinthians 15:45), so that our natural vision does not eclipse the beauty of God's reality.

LEARNING TO SEE AGAIN

Lesson 6 – Leader's Notes

1. The spirit of man can be compared to the eyes of his body since it is the divine instrument for providing light, vision and direction to his soul (Proverbs 20:27). The spirit of the natural man is dark because it is separated from the Father of light and life (Ephesians 4:17-19). Therefore the light of his soul is really darkness (Matthew 6:22, 23), because the god of this world (the devil) has blinded his eyes (spiritual understanding) from seeing the light of the gospel of the glory of Christ (2 Corinthians 4:3, 4).

2. Christ is God's Lamp which gives light to everyone who comes into the world (John 1:4, 5, 9; 8:12). All who are in Christ should walk in fellowship with one another. To do otherwise testifies that they are really children of darkness (1 John 1:5-7). Numberless Christians in this last-day church age (Laodicea), who profess to be walking in the light are living in great deception (Revelation 3:14-22).

3. Spirit vision does not depend on what the natural eyes behold, but only what is authenticated by the faultless Word of God. For those who walk by their inner spirit-man, believing is seeing and not the other way around. Such vision is a blessing (John 20:24-29). Spirit vision also focuses more on what is not seen, than on that which is seen (2 Corinthians 4:17, 18).

4. The inner spirit-man sees by adjusting the short-sighted focus of our natural vision, using the lenses provided by the Word of God. In other words, the Holy Scriptures function as the real eyes of the spirit-man, and defines and shapes his reality. God is the ultimate reality that never changes (Malachi 3:6), and He alone can establish what is, or is not, real, by the power of His Word.

LEARNING TO SEE AGAIN

Lesson 6 – Review Questions

1. What does the book of Proverbs call the spirit of man?

   _____

2. Explain Jesus' paradoxical statement: *If then the light within you is darkness. . .*

   _____

   _____

3. Why is the un-regenerated sinner or religious person unable to see through the things of God although their physical vision is not impaired?

   _____

   _____

4. Why are people unable to see the light of the Gospel of the glory of Jesus Christ?

   _____

   _____

5. What is equivalent to "*walking in the light?*"

   _____

   _____

6. Explain the difference between natural and spiritual vision?

　

　

7. What are the eyes of the spirit-man? How does he see?

　

　

8. For the person who walks by the Spirit, believing is

　

9. How is reality determined in the realm of the spirit?

　

　

10. What we see with our naked eyes is more real and permanent than what we cannot see. True or False?

　

11. Why is God the ultimate reality?

　

13. What are spirit-eyes?

LEARNING TO SEE AGAIN

Lesson 6 – Answer Key

1. The lamp of the Lord. See **Proverbs 20:27.**

2. Through sin, man's spirit became separated from God (the Spirit of Light), so that the lamp of his soul, which was designed to reflect God's light, became darkness instead.

3. Because the inner darkness of their spirit and mind renders them spiritually blind.

4. The god of this world (Satan) has blinded their eyes.

5. Walking by the Spirit.

6. Natural vision is directed by what the eyes see; spiritual vision is directed only by the revelation of the Holy Spirit and the Word of God.

7. The Word of God. He sees, and reckons as real, only what is validated by the Spirit and the Word.

8. Seeing.

9. Only by what God or His Word says.

10. False. Everything we see is passing away. The things of the spiritual realm are eternal. See 2 Corinthians 4:18.

11. He is the only unchangeable force in the universe. He alone can establish what is real by the power of His word.

12. Spirit-eyes are the inner eyes of the soul that gaze unceasingly at God and His Word for clarity and perfection of vision.

LEARNING TO SEE AGAIN

Lesson 6 – Important Scriptures

"The eye is the lamp of the body. If your eyes are good, your whole body will be full of light. ²³But if your eyes are bad, your whole body will be full of darkness. If then the light within you is darkness, how great is that darkness!"
Matthew 6:22, 23

"You will keep on hearing, but will not understand; you will keep on seeing, but will not perceive; ¹⁵For the heart of this people has become dull, and with their ears they scarcely hear, and they have closed their eyes lest they should see with their eyes and hear with their ears, and understand with their heart and return, and I should heal them."
Matthew 13:14, 15

¹⁷This I say therefore, and testify in the Lord, that ye henceforth walk not as other Gentiles walk, in the vanity of their mind, ¹⁸Having the understanding darkened, being alienated from the life of God through the ignorance that is in them, because of the blindness of their heart: ¹⁹Who being past feeling have given themselves over unto lasciviousness, to work all uncleanness with greediness.
Ephesians 4:17-19, KJV

³And even if our gospel is veiled, it is veiled to those who are perishing, ⁴in whose case <u>the god of this world has blinded the minds of the unbelieving so that they might not see the light of the gospel of the glory of Christ</u>, who is the image of God.
2 Corinthians 4:3, 4

"I am the Light of the world; he who follows Me shall not walk in the darkness, but shall have the Light of life."
John 8:12

⁴In him was life; and the life was the light of men. ⁵And the light shineth in darkness; and the darkness comprehended it not. . . ⁹That was the true Light, which lighteth every man that cometh into the world.

John 1:4, 5, 9

²¹*For although they knew God, they neither glorified him as God nor gave thanks to him, but <u>their thinking became futile</u> and <u>their foolish hearts were darkened</u>.* ²²*Although they claimed to be wise, they became fools*

Romans 1:21, 22

⁵*This is the message we have heard from Him and announce to you, that <u>God is Light, and in Him there is no darkness at all</u>.* ⁶*If we say that we have fellowship with Him and yet walk in the darkness, we lie and do not practice the truth;* ⁷*but if we walk in the Light as He Himself is in the Light, we have fellowship with one another, and the blood of Jesus His Son cleanses us from all sin.*

1 John 1:5-7

"To the angel of the church in Laodicea write: The Amen, the faithful and true Witness, the Beginning of the creation of God, says this: ¹⁵*'I know your deeds, that you are neither cold nor hot; I wish that you were cold or hot.* ¹⁶*So because you are lukewarm, and neither hot nor cold, I will spit you out of My mouth.* ¹⁷*Because <u>you say</u>, "<u>I am rich, and have become wealthy, and have need of nothing</u>," and <u>you do not know</u> that <u>you are wretched and miserable and poor and BLIND and naked</u>,* ¹⁸*I advise you to buy from Me gold refined by fire so that you may become rich, and white garments so that you may clothe yourself, and that the shame of your nakedness will not be revealed; and <u>eye salve to anoint your eyes so that you may see</u>.* ¹⁹*Those whom I love, I reprove and discipline; therefore be zealous and repent.* ²⁰*Behold, I stand at the door and knock; if anyone hears My voice and opens the door, I will come in to him and will dine with him, and he with Me.* ²¹*He who overcomes, I will grant to him to sit down with Me on My throne, as I also overcame and sat down with My Father on His throne.* ²²*He who has an ear, let him hear what the Spirit says to the churches.'"*

Revelation 3:14-22

I keep asking that the God of our Lord Jesus Christ, the glorious Father, may give you <u>the Spirit of wisdom and revelation</u>, so <u>that you may know him better</u>. ¹⁸*<u>I pray also that the eyes of your heart may be enlightened</u> in order that you may know the hope to which he has called you, the riches of his glorious inheritance in the saints,*

Ephesians 1:17, 18, NIV

Therefore we do not lose heart, but though our outer man is decaying, yet our inner man is being renewed day by day. ¹⁷For momentary, light affliction is producing for us an eternal weight of glory far beyond all comparison, ¹⁸<u>while we look not at the things which are seen</u>, <u>but at the things which are not seen</u>; <u>for the things which are seen are temporal</u>, <u>but the things which are not seen are eternal</u>.

2 Corinthians 4:16-18

For I am the LORD, I change not; . . .

Malachi 3:6

LEARNING TO SPEAK AGAIN

Chapter 7 – Outline

Then said I, Ah, Lord GOD! behold, I cannot speak: for I am a child.

Jeremiah 1:6

1. **When God created man, He established a direct link between man's spirit and the words proceeding from his mouth.**

    A. Adam's speech pattern was in perfect harmony with his spirit, and with the Great Spirit (God) who shared His life with him.

    B. It was through Satan's deadly breeching of man's spirit and mind that the human race developed speech patterns contrary to the language of heaven and the Word of God.

    C. Satan used man's corrupt speech and the power of his tongue against him and his descendants.

    D. Whatsoever is in a person's spirit (heart) and mind will be made manifest in his speech and actions.

    E. The tongue of the un-regenerated man is lit from the pit of hell and has the power to shape the course of his entire life (James 3:6).

    F. No one, on his own accord, has the ability to tame his own tongue (James 3:7, 8).

2. **Christ provided the sterling example of perfect alignment between the abundant heart (spirit) and the speaking tongue.**

    A. Christ never spoke one unfruitful word because His spirit was perfectly aligned with His tongue and with the will of His Father—the Great Spirit.

B. Everything Christ said came to pass, and everything He prayed for, He received; because His spirit was in unison with that of His Father's.

C. The colossal waves of evil in our world today can be attributed not only to the Ruler of Darkness and his evil hosts, but also to all the negative energy released by the tongues of un-regenerated spirits.

D. It is God's desire to restore perfect alignment between man's spirit and his tongue through the power of the Holy Spirit.

3. **The way to tame a man's tongue is to change the contents of his heart and mind.**

    A. The taming of the human tongue, therefore, must begin with the recreation of man's spirit, and must continue with the disciplining of his mind to obey the guiding influences of the Spirit and the Word of God.

    B. The work of tongue-taming begins with the depositing of the pure milk of the Word in the spirit and mind of the believer.

    C. The renewing of the believer's mind occurs as the combined influences of the Word and the Spirit energizes and strengthens his inner spirit-man.

    D. The Word of God is the divine training tool for the whole spirit, soul and body of the born-again believer—the very source and sustenance of his spirit-life in Christ.

    E. The living Word of God possesses the same power and authority as the Word—Jesus Christ—which brought all of creation into existence.

4. **The born-again believer has the potential to retrieve his speaking ability and authority which was lost through the fall.**

    A. The natural man does not come to the Kingdom of God with the innate ability to speak for or as God.

    B. Only the born-again spirit-man has the potential to speak like God.

C. God must begin the process of filling the born-again believer with His Word, just as He did when He taught Adam to speak at creation.

D. Through the blessings of the New Covenant, God places not only the heavenly deposits in the spirit-life of the believer, but also empowers him to speak the words He places in his mouth, through the Spirit's influence.

E. Through his inner spirit-man the believer must discipline his mind to think and speak the Word of God alone.

F. This spirit which exercises faith in what the Word of God says about all creation must guide the believer to agree with God through the confession of his lips.

5. **Since the life of the child of God is from above, his speech must be in agreement with the Word from heaven.**

   A. As citizens from another country—heaven—the language and lifestyle of the children of God will not harmonize with those of the children of earth.

   B. There are really only two languages in this world—one from the kingdom of heaven above, and one from the kingdom of this world below.

   C. Whatever is born with life from above must speak without embarrassment, the language which reflects that life.

   D. The child of God is under no divine obligation to change the tenor of his language—"water down" his speech—in order to connect and communicate with the un-converted world.

   E. It is the power of God's Spirit, not the giftedness, or flair of our flesh, that would give efficacy to the Word of God in our mouth.

   F. When we, as born-again believers, choose to live by every word that proceeds from our Father's mouth, we will become an unstoppable force for good on the earth.

LEARNING TO SPEAK AGAIN

Lesson 7 – Leader's Notes

1. When God created man, He established a direct link between man's spirit and the words proceeding from his mouth, so that whatever is in a person's heart (spirit or moral center) will be made manifest through his mouth (Matthew 12:34). Man's speech was ordered to manage and control his environment, and, after the fall, the enemy of man used this very powerful phenomenon to wreak havoc in all creation. The tongue of the un-regenerated man became a powerful weapon of destruction, shaping the course of all the chaotic events in people's lives and the world at large (James 3:5-10). Because of sin, man's tongue became a vicious, deadly and un-controllable tool of the evil one.

2, Christ provided the sterling example of perfect alignment between the abundant heart (spirit) and the speaking tongue. Everything Christ said came to pass, and everything He prayed for He received, because His spirit was in unison with that of His Father's (John 12:49, 50). The colossal waves of evil in our world today can be attributed not only to the Ruler of Darkness and his evil hosts, but also to all the negative energy released by the tongues of un-regenerated spirits. However, it is God's will to restore perfect alignment between man's spirit and his tongue through the power of the Spirit and the Word (Deuteronomy 30:11-14; Isaiah 59:21).

3. The only way to tame the human tongue is by changing the contents of the human heart and mind (Jeremiah 31:33, 34), and this begins by depositing the pure milk of the Word in the spirit and mind of the believer. The Word of God is the divine training tool for the whole spirit, soul and body of the born-again believer. It is the very source and sustenance of his spirit-life in Christ (Matthew 4:4).

4. The born-again believer has the potential to retrieve his speaking ability and authority which was lost through the fall. However, it is only the inner spirit of the born-again man that could provide the soul with the potential to speak like God again. Through the blessings of the New Covenant, God places not only the heavenly deposits in the spirit-life of the believer, but also empowers him to speak the words He places in his mouth, through the Spirit's influence (Hebrews 8:10-12). Through his inner spirit-man the

believer must discipline his mind to think and speak the Word of God alone.

5. Since the life of the child of God is from above, his speech must be in agreement with the Word from heaven (Philippians 3:20). There are only two languages in this world—one from the Kingdom of heaven, and the other from the kingdom of earth. The child of God is under no divine obligation to change the tone or theme of His language in order to connect and communicate with the un-converted world (1 John 4:5, 6; John 15:18, 19)). When God's professed children choose to live by every word that proceeds from their Father's mouth, they will become an unstoppable force for good on the earth.

LEARNING TO SPEAK AGAIN

Lesson 7 – Review Questions

1. Describe the influence or impact that the fall of the race had, and continues to have, on mankind's ability to speak.

   _____

   _____

2. What divine principle operates between man's spirit and his speech pattern?

   _____

   _____

3. What power does the Bible says still resides in the human tongue? See **Proverbs 18:21.**

   _____

4. What other deadly influence does the tongue possess? See **James 3:6**

   _____

   _____

5. Who is responsible for giving such deadly influence to the tongue?

   _____

   _____

6. What fountain feeds the river of words released by the tongue?

7. Why is it impossible for man to tame his deadly tongue?

8. How has God made it possible for the believer to tame his tongue?

9. Why were (and are) Jesus' words always fruitful?

10. Why is it imperative for a person to learn how to speak after he/she has been born-again?

11. What should be the sole work of the new believer immediately following his regeneration?

12. Why is it so important for the confession of our mouth to agree with what is written in the Word of God?

13. What is the origin of the two languages which transcends every other language and conversation that operate in our world?

14. What speaking example did Jesus, our elder Brother, leave for us to follow? See **John 12:49, 50.**

15. What is God's ideal for His children, as far as speaking is concerned?

16. What is spirit-tongue?

LEARNING TO SPEAK AGAIN

Lesson 7 – Answer Key

1. Man lost his authority to rule the earth through the power of his speech.

2. God established a direct link between the man's spirit and his speech.

3. Life and death.

4. It can defile a person's entire body and shape the course of his life.

5. Satan and his demon spirits.

6. The "heart"—that is, man's center of spirit and mind.

7. He cannot change the contents of his sin-polluted "heart."

8. Change his moral center by giving him a renewed spirit and mind (also called regeneration). See **Ezekiel 36:26, 27.**

9. His words were always filled with the life-giving energy of His untainted spirit.

10. Because his regenerated spirit has to train his fleshly soul to speak words of life instead of words of death.

11. Fill his spirit and mind with the living Word of God.

12. It's the only way available for us to retrieve authority and power in our speech.

13. The one from above (heaven); the other from below (earth).

14. He spoke the Word of God only—the exact way God wanted Him to do.

15. That they speak only like Him—their Father.

16. Spirit-tongue is the tongue that is directed by the inner spirit-man, and governed by the untainted bit and bridle of the Word and Spirit of God.

LEARNING TO SPEAK AGAIN

Lesson 7 – Important Scriptures

Either make the <u>tree good</u>, and his <u>fruit good</u>; or else make the <u>tree corrupt</u>, and his <u>fruit corrupt</u>: for the tree is known by his fruit. ³⁴O generation of vipers, <u>how can ye, being evil, speak good things</u>? <u>for out of the abundance of the heart the mouth speaketh</u>. ³⁵A good man out of the good treasure of the heart bringeth forth good things: and an evil man out of the evil treasure bringeth forth evil things.

Matthew 12:33-35, KJV

So also the tongue is a small part of the body, and yet it boasts of great things. See how great a forest is set aflame by such a small fire! ⁶And <u>the tongue is a fire</u>, <u>the very world of iniquity</u>; <u>the tongue</u> is set among our members as that which <u>defiles the entire body</u>, and <u>sets on fire the course of our life</u>, and <u>is set on fire by hell</u>. ⁷For every species of beasts and birds, of reptiles and creatures of the sea, is tamed and has been tamed by the human race. ⁸<u>But no one can tame the tongue</u>; <u>it is a restless evil and full of deadly poison</u>. ⁹With it we bless our Lord and Father, and with it we curse men, who have been made in the likeness of God; ¹⁰from the same mouth come both blessing and cursing.

James 3:5-10

For we all stumble in many ways. If anyone does not stumble in what he says, he is a perfect man, able to bridle the whole body as well. ³Now if we put the bits into the horses' mouths so that they will obey us, we direct their entire body as well.

James 3:2, 3

And do not be conformed to this world, but <u>be transformed by the renewing of your mind</u>, so that you may prove what the will of God is, that which is good and acceptable and perfect.

Romans 12:2

Whoever speaks must do so as one speaking the very words of God.

1 Peter 4:11, NRSV

"Man shall not live by bread alone, but by <u>every word</u> that proceeds out of the mouth of God."

Matthew 4:4

"For I did not speak of my own accord, but the Father who sent me <u>commanded me what to say</u> and <u>how to say it</u>. ⁵⁰I know that his command leads to eternal life. So <u>whatever I say is just what the Father has told me to say</u>."

John 12:49, 50

"For this commandment which I command you today is not too difficult for you, nor is it out of reach. ¹²It is not in heaven, that you should say, 'Who will go up to heaven for us to get it for us and make us hear it, that we may observe it?' ¹³"Nor is it beyond the sea, that you should say, 'Who will cross the sea for us to get it for us and make us hear it, that we may observe it?' ¹⁴"<u>But the word is very near you</u>, <u>in your mouth</u> and <u>in your heart</u>, that you may observe it."

Deuteronomy 30:11-14

³³But this shall be the covenant that <u>I will</u> make with the house of Israel; after those days, saith the LORD, <u>I will</u> <u>put my law in their inward parts</u>, and <u>write it in their hearts</u>; and will be their God, and they shall be my people. ³⁴And they shall teach no more every man his neighbour, and every man his brother, saying, Know the LORD: for they shall all know me, from the least of them unto the greatest of them, saith the LORD: for <u>I will</u> forgive their iniquity, and <u>I will</u> remember their sin no more.

Jeremiah 31:33, 34, KJV

They are from the world and therefore speak from the viewpoint of the world, and the world listens to them. ⁶We are from God, and whoever knows God listens to us; but whoever is not from God does not listen to us.

1 John 4:5, 6

For our citizenship is in heaven, from which also we eagerly wait for a Savior, the Lord Jesus Christ.

Philippians 3:20

"If the world hates you, you know that it has hated Me before it hated you. ¹⁹If you

were of the world, the world would love its own; but because you are not of the world, but I chose you out of the world, because of this the world hates you."

John 15:18, 19

"As for Me, this is My covenant with them," says the LORD: "My Spirit which is upon you, and <u>My words which I have put in your mouth shall not depart from your mouth, nor from the mouth of your offspring, nor from the mouth of your offspring's offspring</u>," says the LORD, "from now and forever."

Isaiah 59:21

LEARNING TO WALK AGAIN

Chapter 8 – Outline

If we live by the Spirit, let us also walk by the Spirit.

Galatians 5:25

1. **In biblical terms, "walking" refers primarily to the way in which an individual conducts himself in all his daily affairs and in his interactions with others.**

   A. An individual's "walking" is governed by his ability (or inability) to take control of his thought-life and the cravings of his flesh.

   B. Mankind can walk in two ways—according to the broad ways of the world (from below), or according to the narrow way of the Kingdom of God (from above); according to the flesh, or according to the spirit.

   C. Those who choose to live by the philosophies of the world are "walking" under the influence of the prince of the power of the air, and are demonized or in-bred by spirits of disobedience.

   D. The masses of humanity are quite ignorant of the magnitude of the influence that Satan and his evil angels exert on their lives.

2. **Walking by the Spirit is the only reliable way to counteract the power and cravings of the flesh.**

   A. Jesus is not only the *way* called *narrow*, which leads to the Father and eternal life; He is also the only door or *gate* called *strait*.

   B. All those who enter the *narrow way* must relinquish completely everything that pertains to the *broad way* of the world.

   C. "Walking" in the *narrow way* calls for more than minor "here or there" adjustments to attitudes and lifestyle.

D. The inner-man of the of the believer's spirit is capable of "walking" successfully in the *narrow way* because he is created in the righteous and holy image of God.

E. "Walking" by the Spirit means "walking" under the complete authority of the Word of God.

3. **Learning to "walk" again in the *narrow way* calls for laying aside all the "weights" associated with the old life of sin.**

    A. Keeping one's attention focused on Jesus is the key to "walking" successfully in the *narrow way* and to completing the course that leads to eternal life.

    B. Jesus left all believers an example of self-denial and obedience through the things which he suffered, leaving the total outcome of his life in the hands of the Father (1 Peter 2:21-23; Hebrews 5:8).

    C. All Christians must prepare themselves to suffer in their flesh if they are going to be true followers of Jesus.

    D. Self-denial and fleshly suffering are heaven's ordained means for training the believer to "walk" in the *narrow way*.

4. **The born-again believer must learn to "walk" by faith and not by sight—what he perceives through his senses.**

    A. Only spirit-life is capable of "walking" by the Holy Spirit of God, and in complete victory over the desires of the flesh.

    B. The ability to walk in the natural sense is based on developmental or physiological factors; but walking by the Spirit is strictly a faith-based experience.

    C. There are fundamental differences between a life that is lived based on facts and a life that is lived by faith in God alone.

    D. Facts tend to hide the truth of our situations, for we often fail to comprehend their true meaning or purpose.

E. Through faith in God and He who abides in us, we are able to overcome all the evil forces in the world.

5. **In this spiritual "walk," the children of God must be armed to fight the evil forces of darkness.**

    A. Believers cannot fight spiritual warfare with carnal weapons and expect victory.

    B. Our spiritual weapons are mighty only through God, and not ourselves.

    C. The shield of faith and the Sword of the Spirit are indispensable offensive and defensive weapons for the warfare against the hosts of darkness.

    D. The substance and the evidence on which faith is grounded is the unfailing Word of God.

    E. Our faith becomes an impregnable shield when we place our mind and thoughts under the authoritative Word of the Almighty.

    F. Believers must elevate the Word of God from the common status of being simply a textbook for church services to the lofty heights of being an indispensable life-book, governing our every thought and action.

6. **To walk in victory, the born-again believer must learn to live his life based only on the truth, and not on mere facts.**

    A. Facts are based on concrete experiences guided by human reason; truth is based on faith supported only by the Word of God.

    B. Only what the Bible says is true, really IS, regardless of the nature of the facts that are present.

    C. Everything is not what it seems to be when God is in the picture.

    D. Facts are fleeting and changeable, but truth is everlasting and changeless.

    E. The facts of our situation is seldom—if at all—the truth of our situation.

F. For the inner spirit-man, facts always lead to bondage, but truth always leads to freedom.

G. The over-arching truth for the child of God who is learning to "walk" again is that his heavenly Father is working mysteriously in all the facts of his life for his present and eternal good.

LEARNING TO WALK AGAIN

Lesson 8 – Teacher's Notes

1. In biblical terms, "walking" refers primarily to the way in which an individual conducts himself in all of his daily affairs, and in all of his interactions with others. There are only two ways available for all to walk—the broad way of the world (from below), or the narrow way of the Kingdom of God (from above); according to the flesh, or according to the spirit (Matthew 7:13, 14). All those who choose to live (walk) by the philosophies of the world are "walking" under the influence of the prince of the power of the air, and are demonized or in-bred by spirits of disobedience (Ephesians 2:1-3). The masses of humanity are totally ignorant about the magnitude of the influence that the powers of darkness exert on their daily lives.

2. Walking by the Spirit is the only reliable way to counteract the powerful cravings of the flesh (Galatians 5:16). Pursuing this walk and living life in the narrow way are one and the same experience. All who enter this walk must relinquish completely everything that pertains to the broad way of the world. Walking by the Spirit means walking under the full authority of the Word of God.

3. Learning to "walk" again in the narrow way calls for laying aside all the "weights" associated with the old life of sin and keeping one's eyes fixed on Jesus (Hebrews 12:1, 2). This is a walk of self-denial and suffering from which none of God's children are exempt (1 Peter 4:1, 2; Hebrews 12:7-11).

4. The born-again believer must learn how to "walk" by the Spirit through faith, and not by the sight or the organs of his senses (2 Corinthians 5:7). It is only spirit-life that is capable of "walking" under the direction of the Holy Spirit of God (Romans 8:16), and in complete victory over the evil craving of the natural self. Walking in the natural sense depends on developmental and psychological factors; but walking by the Spirit is strictly a faith-based experience.

5. In his spiritual "walk," the believer must be armed to fight the evil forces of darkness, and he cannot fight spiritual warfare with natural (or carnal) weapons (Ephesians 6:12). Just as the born-again man is spiritual, so are

the weapons with which he must wage war with evil forces (2 Corinthians 10:4). His fight is successful whenever he fights by faith in the power greater than himself—God (1 Timothy 6:12). Our faith becomes an impregnable and mighty weapon when we place our mind and thoughts under the authoritative Word of the Almighty.

6. To "walk" in victory, the child of God must learn to live his entire life based only on the truth and not on mere facts. Truth is grounded in faith in God and His Word; facts are base on one's perception of reality that is experienced or imagined. Facts can change at any given moment, but truth abides forever—like God who alone defines what truth is. Only what God says is true. The facts of our situation is seldom—if at all—the truth about our situation. For the inner spirit-man, facts always lead to bondage, but truth always lead to freedom. The most amazing, over-arching truth of all is that God is always working out all the situations in His children's lives for their good (Romans 8:28).

LEARNING TO WALK AGAIN

Lesson 8 – Review Questions

1. What is the biblical understanding of the term *walk*?

   _____

   _____

2. What are the only two ways available for an individual to conduct his life in this world?

   _____

   _____

3. What great truth is implied in Jesus' invitation to *enter in at the strait gate*?

   _____

   _____

4. What spiritual influences propel those who choose to walk in the broad way, according to the course of this world?

   _____

   _____

5. Why is it necessary for the believer to learn how to walk again?

   _____

6. What reverse dynamics operate between the believer's spirit and his flesh in his daily walk?

_____

_____

7. What is the purpose of fleshly suffering in the spiritual walk?

_____

_____

8. In Hebrews 12, what does God call those who reject fleshly chastisement (suffering), yet professing to be His children?

_____

9. In the same chapter, God calls Himself the Father of what type of children?

_____

10. As a Son of man, how did Jesus learn obedience?

_____

_____

11. Walking by faith and walking by the Spirit is one and the same walk. True or False?

_____

12. Walking by faith and walking under the full authority of the Word of God is one and the same experience. True or False?

13. As far as the spirit-man is concerned, what is truth?

14. Give one significant difference between facts and truth explained in this book.

15. By what rule must the believer live, who is learning to walk again—that is by the Spirit?

16. What are spirit-feet?

LEARNING TO WALK AGAIN

Lesson 8 – Answer Key

1. The way in which an individual conducts himself in all his daily affairs and in his interactions with others.

2. According to the ways of the world (from below), or as citizens of the Kingdom of God (from above); **OR** according to the flesh, or by the Spirit of God; **OR** according to the dictates of one's thoughts and emotions (by sight), or by the Word of the Living God (by faith).

3. Mankind has only one choice since, by default (Adam's sin), all humanity is already living in the broad way.

4. Satan and demon spirits.

5. Because walking by the Spirit is the total opposite to walking by the flesh or "self."

6. Whatever is done to one has the reverse effect on the other——for example: One has to die (flesh) for the other to live (spirit); nourishing one weakens the other; denying one embraces the other; defending one threatens the other; and supporting one diminishes the other.

7. To strip the flesh of its tenacious power. See **1 Peter 4:1, 2; James 1:2-4.**

8. Bastards or illegitimate.

9. Spirits—not flesh.

10. Through the things which He suffered in His flesh. See **Hebrews 5:8; 2:10.**

11. True.

12. True

13. Truth is only what God or His Word declares.

14. Facts can change, but truth is eternal as the God of truth is.

15. Live (really, walk) by every word of God—that is, the Truth.

16. Spirit-feet are faith-directed feet that are governed by only the Spirit and the Word, and not the wisdom and understanding of man.

LEARNING TO WALK AGAIN

Lesson 8 – Important Scriptures

If we live by the Spirit, let us also walk by the Spirit.

Galatians 5:25

¹³Enter ye in at the strait gate: for <u>wide is the gate</u>, and <u>broad is the way</u>, that leadeth to destruction, and many there be which go in thereat: ¹⁴Because <u>strait is the gate</u>, and <u>narrow is the way</u>, which leadeth unto life, and few there be that find it.

Matthew 7:13, 14, KJV

¹And you were dead in your trespasses and sins, ²in which <u>you formerly walked according to the course of this world</u>, <u>according to the prince of the power of the air</u>, <u>of the spirit that is now working in the sons of disobedience</u>. ³Among them we too all formerly lived in the lusts of our flesh, indulging the desires of the flesh and of the mind, and were by nature <u>children of wrath</u>, even as the rest.

Ephesians 2:1-3

So this I say, and affirm together with the Lord, that you walk no longer just as the Gentiles also walk, in the futility of their mind, ¹⁸being darkened in their understanding, excluded from the life of God because of the ignorance that is in them, because of the hardness of their heart; ¹⁹and they, having become callous, have given themselves over to sensuality for the practice of every kind of impurity with greediness.

Ephesians 4:17-19

⁶For all that is in the world, the lust of the flesh and the lust of the eyes and the boastful pride of life, is not from the Father, but is from the world. ¹⁷The world is passing away, and also its lusts; but the one who does the will of God lives forever.

1 John 2:16, 17

But I say, walk by the Spirit, and you will not carry out the desire of the flesh.

Galatians 5:16

"I am the door; if anyone enters through Me, he will be saved, and will go in and out and find pasture.

John 10:9

. . . you did not learn Christ in this way, ²¹if indeed you have heard Him and have been taught in Him, just as truth is in Jesus, ²²that, in reference to your former manner of life, you lay aside the old self, which is being corrupted in accordance with the lusts of deceit, ²³and that you be renewed in the spirit of your mind, ²⁴and put on the new self, which in the likeness of God has been created in righteousness and holiness of the truth.

Ephesians 4:20-24

they that are after the flesh do mind the things of the flesh; but they that are after the Spirit, the things of the Spirit.

Romans 8:5, KJV

Trust in the LORD with all thine heart and lean not unto thine own understanding. ⁶In all thy ways acknowledge Him, and He shall direct thy paths.

Proverbs 3:5, 6, KJV

Therefore I, the prisoner of the Lord, implore you to walk in a manner worthy of the calling with which you have been called, ²with all <u>humility</u> and <u>gentleness</u>, with <u>patience</u>, <u>showing tolerance for one another in love</u>, ³being diligent to <u>preserve the unity of the Spirit</u> in the bond of peace.

Ephesians 4:1-3

Therefore, since we have so great a cloud of witnesses surrounding us, let us also <u>lay aside every encumbrance</u> and <u>the sin which so easily entangles us</u>, and let us run with endurance the race that is set before us, ² fixing our eyes on Jesus, <u>the author and perfecter of faith</u>, who for the joy set before Him endured the cross, despising the shame, and has sat down at the right hand of the throne of God. ³For <u>consider Him</u> who has endured such hostility by sinners against Himself, <u>so that you will not grow weary and lose heart</u>.

Hebrews 12:1-3

Therefore, since Christ has suffered in the flesh, <u>arm yourselves also with the same purpose</u>, because <u>he who has suffered in the flesh has ceased from sin</u>, ²so as to live the rest of the time in the flesh no longer for the lusts of men, but for the will of God.

1 Peter 4:1-2

If ye endure chastening, God dealeth with you as with sons; for what son is he whom the father chasteneth not? ⁸But <u>if ye be without chastisement</u>, whereof all are partakers, <u>then are ye bastards</u>, and not sons. ⁹Furthermore we have had fathers of our flesh which corrected us, and we gave them reverence: shall we not much rather be in subjection unto the Father of spirits, and live? ¹⁰For they verily for a few days chastened us after their own pleasure; but he for our profit, <u>that we might be partakers of his holiness</u>. ¹¹Now no chastening for the present seemeth to be joyous, but grievous: nevertheless afterward it yieldeth the peaceable fruit of righteousness unto them which are exercised thereby.

Hebrews 12:7-11, KJV

Who in the days of his flesh, when he had offered up prayers and supplications with strong crying and tears unto him that was able to save him from death, and was heard in that he feared; ⁸Though he were a Son, <u>yet learned he obedience by the things which he suffered</u>; ⁹And being made perfect, he became the author of eternal salvation unto all them that obey him.

Hebrews 5:7-9

For our struggle is not against flesh and blood, but against the rulers, against the powers, against the world forces of this darkness, against the spiritual forces of wickedness in the heavenly.

Ephesians 6:12

Fight the good fight of faith; take hold of the eternal life to which you were called. . .

1 Timothy 6:12

For though we walk in the flesh, we do not war after the flesh: ⁴(For <u>the weapons of our warfare are</u> not carnal, but <u>mighty through God</u> to the pulling down of strong holds;) ⁵<u>Casting down imaginations</u>, and every high thing that exalteth itself against *the knowledge of God, and <u>bringing into captivity every thought</u> to the obedience of Christ.*

2 Corinthians 10:3-5

And we know that God causes all things to work together for good to those who love God, to those who are called according to His purpose.

Romans 8:28

PART III

LIKE FATHER LIKE SON

Be imitators of God, therefore, as dearly loved children and live a life of love . . .

Ephesians 5:1, 2, NIV

I am the way, and the truth, and the life . . .

John 14:6

LIVING GOD'S LIFE

Chapter 9 – Outline

"It is written, 'man shall not live on bread alone, but <u>on every word</u> that proceeds out <u>of the mouth of God</u>."

Matthew 4:4

1. **Living God's life starts with making the most important life-choice.**

   A. Kingdom citizenship requires all potential subjects to make a choice regarding kingship loyalty.

   B. Once a person has entered the strait gate (Jesus Christ) that leads to life in the Kingdom, he must make the second choice to choose the life of God over his own.

   C. One cannot live successfully by catering for spirit and flesh life at the same time.

   D. In order to live God's life, the child of God must totally relinquish his own—the one he inherited through Adam.

2. **It takes spirit-life to reflect or imitate the Spirit life of God.**

   A. It is God's purpose that the crucifixion of the cross be transferred, by faith, into the daily experience of the believer.

   B. The experience of the cross is a daily denying of self, which is a far cry from the self-indulgent Christianity that characterizes our age.

   C. Living God's life involves making the daily choice to put to death the deeds of the flesh that are characteristic of our old self.

   D. It is through the crucifixion of our flesh that we really live in the spirit.

   E. As we patiently carry our cross for crucifixion, the life of God graciously unfolds in our spirit.

F. The only way to release the power of God's life in ourselves, is through the destruction of the devil's seed which resides in our flesh.

3. **The yoke of Christ represents oneness of spirit, uniting the incorruptible seed of the believer's spirit with His divine substitute, the Holy Spirit of promise.**

    A. The yoke of Christ is established through the Holy Spirit who dwells within our spirit.

    B. If humanity does not resist His grace through fleshly strivings, He will redeem all from the "guttermost," and save all to the uttermost.

    C. The only work that God expects of humanity is to believe in Jesus, and to surrender to that belief.

    D. When we learn to submit and surrender to every word that proceeds from the mouth of God, then we would discover the amazing secret of His life in our spirit.

4. **Because we are one with Christ in spirit, we can learn from His example, while being empowered by His victorious life from within.**

    A. Christ learned obedience through the things which He suffered (Hebrews 5:8).

    B. Christ became the imitator of man so that men might become the imitators of God. He lived like men so that men might live like God.

    C. We can only possess the mind and attitude of Christ when our flesh, like His, has been taken to the wilderness, to be stripped completely of all pride, arrogance and self-conceit.

    D. We will never be able to find rest for their souls until self has experienced the wilderness of deprivation, temptation and trial; the Gethsemane of abandonment, loneliness and doubt; and the separation and death of Calvary.

    E. Our spiritual lives remain in continual turmoil because the enemy has deceived us into living a life that is devoted to self and its fleshly ways.

F. The only way to find rest for your soul is through the crucifixion of the flesh.

5. Christ, "the Light," came to reveal the God who is called "Light."

A. Without Christ's revelation of the Father, the whole world would have been in total darkness with regard to its knowledge of the immortal, invisible, eternal and only wise God.

B. God is light and there is absolutely no darkness or shadiness in Him.

C. Christ came from the God of Light to be the Light of the world.

D. If we walk in the Light (in Christ and His Word), it testifies to the fact that we have fellowship with God, the Father of lights.

E. Walking in the Light is the same as walking in the life of God.

6. Christ is the bridge permanently linking humanity with Divinity, and Divinity with humanity.

A. Christ's mission demanded that the Savior immerse Himself in the life of man and the life of God all at the same time.

B. That meant Christ first had to immerse Himself in man—that is, He became man; and then, as man, to immerse Himself in God—that is, He lived like God.

C. Christ is the God-man and the man-God; the Son of God and the Son of man.

D. Christ was not only God in man, but He was also man in God. He did not only reveal God to men, He demonstrated how men could live like God.

E. The Savior was NEVER self-driven. He was always God-driven. He lived His life in total surrender to His Father's will.

F. The Savior lived a very simple and consistent life of ministry and communion—a life that made contact with men and enjoyed fellowship with God.

- G. When our will is yielded to the point where we live and function only by the dictates of God's will and His Word, then the power which attended Jesus will be fully released to operate in and through us.

- H. This is the heart of what salvation is all about—God being able to express His total will through the surrendered will of man.

7. **Just as Christ represented and imitated the Father, so the Holy Spirit represents and imitates Christ.**

   - A. Both Christ and the Holy Spirit were divinely appointed to the position of Counselor, Advocate (like a lawyer) and Helper for the spiritual nurture of God's children.

   - B. The Holy Spirit is the imitation of Jesus for all believers. He will execute precisely what Jesus instructs Him to do and to say.

8. **As God's children, we share His nature in our spirits, and have been fully equipped to imitate Him as our Father.**

   - A. God's Holy Spirit bears confirmation to our spirit that we are indeed the children of God.

   - B. We can live like God because we have the life of God abiding in us, through the God-man (God in man or God living like men), Jesus Christ.

   - C. Many who claim to be children of God would be sadly disappointed, because they do not carry any visible evidence of His dominant gene—LOVE.

   - D. The individual who does not love his fellow man does not know God.

   - E. We share God's Spirit of love because God dwells in our spirit and we dwell in His.

   - F. One simply cannot be in God, and God in him, without being obedient to the Word of God.

9. **God's children must mirror His perfection to the world through love and unity.**

    A. Ultimately, living God's life means living a life of love; and to live a life of love means living God's Word.

    B. Life's most important, existential choice is that of bringing my thought-life under the full authority of the Bible.

    C. God's perfection comes ONLY from His Mystery within our spirit—Jesus Christ, our hope of glory (Colossians 1:26, 27; 2:2).

    D. We must quit struggling with our "old Adam" model that is destined for destruction, and let our inner spirit-man "rip"!

LIVING GOD'S LIFE

Lesson 9 – Leader's Notes

1. Living God's life starts with making the most important life-choice regarding kingdoms (Light and darkness) and masters—God and material wealth (Matthew 6:24). One cannot be loyal to both masters, or kingdoms at the same time. He must make the choice between one, or the other. In order to live God's life, the believer of necessity must relinquish his own.

2. It takes spirit-life to perfectly reflect or imitate the Spirit-life of God. This spirit-life functions as the controlling influence of the believer's natural life, which diminishes daily through self-denial. It is God's purpose that the crucifixion of the cross be transferred, by faith, into the daily experience of the believer (Galatians 2:20; Romans 6:5-14). It is through crucifixion of our flesh that we really live—not die—in the spirit (Romans 8:13, 14). The only way to release the power of God's life in us is through the destruction of the devil's seed which resides in our flesh.

3. The yoke which Christ calls all His disciples to bear is oneness of spirit with Him, uniting the incorruptible seed of the believer's spirit with His divine Substitute, the Holy Spirit of promise (Matthew 11:29, 30; 1 Corinthians 6:17). If we do not resist His grace through our fleshly strivings, deviant thoughts and selfish desires, Christ will redeem us from the "guttermost" and save all to the uttermost. The only work that God expects of humanity is to believe in Jesus and to surrender to that belief (John 6:28, 29).

4. Because we are one with Christ in spirit, we can learn from His example, while being empowered by His victorious life from within. Christ learned obedience through the things which He suffered in the flesh (Hebrews 5:8) and so would we (1 Peter 4:1, 2). Christ became the imitator of man so that men might become the imitators of God. He lived like men so that men might live like God. We can only possess the mind and attitude of Christ (Philippians 2:5-8) when our flesh, like His, has been taken to the wilderness, to be stripped completely of all pride, arrogance and self-conceit. The only way for us to find rest for our souls is by putting self and flesh to rest through crucifixion.

5. Christ, the Light, came to reveal the God who is also called Light (1 John

1:5), and the Father of lights (James 1:17). If we walk in the Light (in Christ and His Word), it bears witness to the fact that we have fellowship with God, the Father of lights. Walking in the Light is the same as walking in the life of God.

6. Christ is the bridge which permanently links humanity with Divinity, and Divinity with humanity. He immersed Himself in the life of man and in the life of God at the same time. As the God-man, He wrapped Himself in humanity; and as the man-God, He showed how men could live the life of God. Christ was never self-driven, but always God driven. He lived His entire life in total surrender to His Father's will (John 5:19, 30; 12:49, 50). The heart of salvation could be summarized as God being able to express His will through the surrendered will of man.

7. Just as Christ represented and imitated the Father, so the Holy Spirit represents and imitates Christ. Both Christ and the Holy Spirit were divinely appointed to the position of Counselor, Advocate (like a lawyer) and Helper for the spiritual nurture of God's children (John 14:16, 17). The Holy Spirit is the imitation of Jesus for all believers. He will execute precisely what Jesus instructs Him to do and to say (John 16:13, 14).

8. As God's children, we share His nature in our spirits, and have been fully equipped to imitate Him as our Father (2 Peter 1:3, 4; Ephesians 4:24; 5:1, 2). God's Holy Spirit confirms that we are indeed God's children (Romans 8:16), and as such, we can imitate our Father through the life of His Son living in us. Many who claim to be children of God fail His paternity test because they do not have His love in themselves (1 John 4:7, 8). We share God's spirit of love because He dwells in our spirit and we dwell in His (1 John 4:13, 16). Obedience is the fruit that testifies to the love of God in all His children (1 John 5:2, 3; John 15:10).

9. God's children must mirror His perfection to the world through love and unity (Matthew 5:48). Ultimately, living God's life means living a life of love; and to live a life of love means living God's Word. The perfection of God's life comes ONLY from His Mystery (Jesus Christ) abiding within our spirits—that is, Jesus Christ, our hope of glory (Colossians 1:26, 27; 2:2). Therefore, we must quit struggling with our "old Adam" model that is destined for destruction, give full and free rein to our inner spirit-man.

LIVING GOD'S LIFE

Lesson 9 – Review Questions

1. What important choice must the believer make after choosing to enter the strait gate that leads to the narrow way?.

   _____

   _____

2. Why is it impossible for the new believer to imitate Christ through the power of his natural life?

   _____

   _____

3. What is the yoke that Christ has called all His followers to bear?

   _____

4. Why is it so difficult for many believers to find rest for their souls?

   _____

5. What is the "work of God" that He expects of all believers?

   _____

6. Complete the sentence: Christ became the imitation of man so that men can become

   _____

7. What is the motive force that drives the self-centered systems of our world?

8. What is the only way for a believer to find peace and rest for his soul?

9. What was Christ's secret for being the perfect imitation of His father?

10. What enduring principle expresses the very heart of what salvation is all about?

11. Why is it possible for believers to live the life of God?

12. How is it possible for believers to imitate God's life?

13. What does one's ability to love others have to do with living the life of God?

14. Ultimately, what does living God's life really mean?

_____

_____

15. What must the believer do to mirror God's perfection?

_____

_____

LIVING GOD'S LIFE

Lesson 9 – Answer Key

1. Choose to live God's life over his own—that is, let the Christ in him live, while denying the "I" in himself. See **Galatians 2:20.**

2. Only spirit life can imitate the Spirit life of God in Jesus. Natural cannot imitate spiritual.

3. Oneness of spirit—Christ's Spirit with ours. See **1 Corinthians 6:17.**

4. They try to live from self more than from the Christ in them.

5. Believe and surrender.

6. The imitators of God.

7. Eating from the tree of the knowledge of good and evil.

8. Put self and flesh to rest through daily denial and crucifixion.

9. He was never self-driven. He was always God-driven.

10. God being able to express His total will through the surrendered will of man.

11. Because they carry the incorruptible seed of God's life within themselves.

12. By feeding and nurturing the God's incorruptible seed-life.

13. It confirms the reality of God's life within. It's God's paternity test.

14. Living a life of love.

15. Detach himself from his old way of being, thinking and doing, and live by every word of God

LIVING GOD'S LIFE

Lesson 9 – Important Scriptures

"No man can serve two masters: for either he will hate the one, and love the other; or else he will hold to the one, and despise the other. Ye cannot serve God and mammon."

Matthew 6:24, KJV

"He who loves his life loses it, and he who hates his life in this world will keep it to life eternal."

John 12:25

"I have been crucified with Christ; and it is no longer I who live, but Christ lives in me; and the life which I now live in the flesh I live by faith in the Son of God, who loved me and gave Himself up for me."

Galatians 2:20

"For if we have become united with Him in the likeness of His death, certainly we shall also be in the likeness of His resurrection, ⁶knowing this, that our old self was crucified with Him, in order that our body of sin might be done away with, so that we would no longer be slaves to sin; ⁷for he who has died is freed from sin.

⁸Now if we have died with Christ, we believe that we shall also live with Him, ⁹knowing that Christ, having been raised from the dead, is never to die again; death no longer is master over Him. ¹⁰For the death that He died, He died to sin once for all; but the life that He lives, He lives to God.

*¹¹Even so **consider yourselves to be dead to sin**, but alive to God in Christ Jesus. ¹²Therefore **do not let sin reign** in your mortal body so that you obey its lusts, ¹³and **do not go on presenting** the members of your body to sin as instruments of unrighteousness; but **present yourselves to God** as those alive from the dead, and your members as instruments of righteousness to God. ¹⁴For **sin shall not be master over you**, for you are not under law but under grace."*

Romans 6:5-14, emphasis mine

for if you are living [or choose to live] according to the flesh, you must die; but if <u>by the Spirit</u> you are <u>putting to death the deeds of the body</u>, you will live. ^{14}For all who are being led by the Spirit of God, these are sons of God.
Romans 8:13, 14 [brackets mine]

"Take My yoke upon you and learn from Me for I am gentle and humble in heart; and you will find rest for your souls. ^{30}For My yoke is easy and My burden is light."
Matthew 11:29, 30

But the one who joins himself to the Lord is one spirit with Him.
1 Corinthians 6:17

Therefore they said to Him, "What shall we do, so that we may work the <u>works of God</u>?" ^{29}Jesus answered and said to them, "This is the <u>work of God</u>, that you believe in Him whom He has sent."
John 6:28, 29

Though he were a Son, yet learned he obedience by the things which he suffered.
Hebrews 5:8

Forasmuch then as Christ hath suffered for us in the flesh, arm yourselves likewise with the same mind: for he that hath suffered in the flesh hath ceased from sin; ^{2}That he no longer should live the rest of his time in the flesh to the lusts of men, but to the will of God.
1 Peter 4:1, 2

Have this attitude in yourselves which was also in Christ Jesus, ^{6}who, although He existed in the form of God, did not regard equality with God a thing to be grasped, ^{7}but emptied Himself, taking the form of a bond-servant, and being made in the likeness of men. ^{8}Being found in appearance as a man, He humbled Himself by becoming obedient to the point of death, even death on a cross.
Philippians 2:5-8

This then is the message which we have heard of him, and declare unto you, that

God is light, and in him is no darkness at all.

1 John 1:5

Every good gift and every perfect gift is from above, and cometh down from the Father of lights, with whom is no variableness, neither shadow of turning.

James 1:17

"I tell you the truth, the Son can do nothing by himself; he can do only what he sees his Father doing, because whatever the Father does the Son also does."

John 5:19, NIV

I can of mine own self do nothing: <u>as I hear, I judge</u>: and my judgment is just; because I seek not mine own will, but the will of the Father which hath sent me.

John 5:30

For I did not speak of my own accord, but <u>the Father</u> who sent me <u>commanded me what to say and how to say it</u>. ⁵⁰I know that his command leads to eternal life. <u>So whatever I say is just what the Father has told me to say</u>."

John 12:49, 50, NIV

But so much the more went there a fame abroad of him: and great multitudes came together to hear, and to be healed by him of their infirmities. ¹⁶And <u>he withdrew himself into the wilderness</u>, and <u>prayed</u>.

Luke 5:15, 16

*But when he, the Spirit of truth, comes, he will guide you into all truth. <u>He will not speak on his own; he will speak **only** what he hears</u>, and he will tell you what is yet to come. ¹⁴He will bring glory to me by <u>taking from what is mine and making it known to you</u>.*

John 16:13, 14, NIV

And I will pray the Father, and he shall give you <u>another Comforter</u>, that he may abide with you forever; ¹⁷<u>Even the Spirit of truth</u>; whom the world cannot receive, because it seeth him not, neither knoweth him: but ye know him; for he dwelleth *with you, and shall be in you.*

John 14:16, 17

According as his divine power hath given unto us all things that pertain unto life and godliness, through the knowledge of him that hath called us to glory and virtue: ⁴Whereby are given unto us exceeding great and precious promises: that by these ye might be partakers of the divine nature, having escaped the corruption that is in the world through lust.

2 Peter 1:3, 4

And that ye put on the new man, which after God is created in righteousness and true holiness.

Ephesians 4:24

Therefore be imitators of God, as beloved children; ²and <u>walk in love</u>, . . . ⁸for you were formerly darkness, but now you are Light in the Lord; <u>walk as children of Light</u>.

Ephesians 5:1, 2, 8

Beloved, let us love one another, for <u>love is from God</u>; and <u>everyone who loves is born of God</u> and <u>knows God</u>. ⁸The one who does not love does not know God, for God is love.

1 John 4:7, 8

by this we know that we abide in Him and He in us, because He has given us of His Spirit . . . and the one who abides in love abides in God, and God abides in him.

1 John 4:13, 16

By this we know that we have come to know Him, if we keep His commandments. ⁴The one who says, "I have come to know Him," and does not keep His commandments, is a liar, and the truth is not in him; ⁵but <u>whoever keeps His word, in him the love of God has truly been perfected. By this we know that we are in Him</u>:

1 John 2:3-5

"If you keep My commandments, you will abide in My love; just as I have kept My Father's commandments and abide in His love."

John 15:10

By this we know that we love the children of God, when we love God and observe His commandments. ³<u>For this is the love of God</u>, <u>that we keep His commandments</u>; and His commandments are not burdensome.

1 John 5:2, 3

"Be ye therefore, perfect even as your Father in heaven is perfect"

Matthew 5:48

²⁶Even the mystery which hath been hid from ages and from generations, but now is made manifest to his saints: ²⁷To whom God would make known what is the riches of the glory of this mystery among the Gentiles; which is Christ in you, the hope of glory:

Colossians 1:26, 27

I want their hearts to be encouraged and united in love, so that they may have all the riches of assured understanding and have the knowledge of God's mystery, that is, Christ himself.

Colossians 2:2, NRSV

Contact Information

Dr. Ruthven J. Roy

NETWORK DISCIPLING MINISTRIES
P.O. Box 33
Berrien Springs, MI 49103

Tel: (301) 514-2383
Email: ruthvenroy@networkdiscipling.org
Website: www.networkdiscipling.org

www.ingramcontent.com/pod-product-compliance
Lightning Source LLC
Chambersburg PA
CBHW081457040426
42446CB00016B/3288